DISCONNECT

30 days to break free from phone addiction

1 – INTRODUCTION

DISCONNECT

30 days to break free from phone addiction

Copyright © 2025 Dr. Violeta Noriel

All rights reserved.

ISBN: 9798319173058

INDEX

INTRODUCTION 5
   About the author.. 6
   Why did I write this book?... 7
   My story (and that of my family)... 9

PART ONE - AWARENESS RAISING 11
   Are you addicted to your cell phone? Take the test!............ 12
   What your cell phone is doing to your brain (and your life)......... 16
   The big con: Why you can't let go of your cell phone 23

PART TWO - THE 30-DAY CHALLENGE 27
   How does the plan work?... 28
   Week 1 - Take control.. 31
   Week 2 - Cut the chains... 49
   Week 3 - Replace the habit.. 67
   Week 4 - Consolidate the change.. 88

PART THREE - RESOURCES TO HELP YOU MOVE FORWARD 125
   The challenge is over... but the road continues.................. 126
   Your maintenance plan 127
   Useful resources 131
   Quick guide for parents: How to help your children unwind...... 135
   What you should never forget.. 139
   This is as far as we have come 141
   Notes and reflections 143

INTRODUCTION

ABOUT THE AUTHOR

Dr. Violeta Noriel is a psychologist with over 20 years of experience in addiction treatment. After seeing how phone addiction was affecting not only her patients, but also her own family, she decided to apply everything she had learned to the digital world. The result is this book: a close, honest and practical guide for anyone who wants to take back control of their time, their attention and their life.

She writes not from a place of superiority, but from shared experience. And she'll be by your side through every step of this 30-day journey.

WHY DID I WRITE THIS BOOK?

You may be surprised to know that this book is not written by someone who has always lived "disconnected". Quite the contrary. I have been a psychologist specializing in addictions for more than twenty years, and even so, I have also fallen into the cell phone trap. And it's not just me: my two teenage sons have spent years glued to their screens, and my mother, who is over 70, spends her days jumping from one application to another as if her life depended on it.

So when I tell you that I know what you're going through, believe me: **I do**.

This book is born from my professional experience, but also from my own personal and family struggles. I have seen hundreds of people get lost inside a screen and waste hours of their day.

But, more importantly, I've seen hundreds more regain control. And I want you to be one of them.

This isn't a typical self-help book. I'm not going to tell you to throw your phone in the trash or to go live in the country. You will not find empty phrases or magic promises.

What you will find is <u>a real and effective method to regain control of your life in just 30 days</u>. A practical, direct and empathetic plan, based on my clinical experience and on real cases of people like you who, one day, decided to stop being slaves of their cell phone.

In addition, you will read stories of patients who have overcome their addiction, anecdotes from my own family, facts that will open your eyes and, above all, a clear path so that you too can get out of this.

What do you need to start this challenge?

You don't need infinite willpower.

You don't need to leave your cell phone in a drawer forever.

You only need two things: **commitment and the will to get your time, your attention and your life back.**

If you've made it this far, you've already taken the first step. The second is to join me for the next 30 days. Some days will cost you. Others will surprise you. But I promise you one thing: if you follow the plan, when you finish this book you won't be the same person who started it.

Important notice: It's not magic, it's commitment

This is not a quick trick or an instant solution. Getting unhooked from your cell phone takes time, effort and, above all, honesty with yourself. But I also assure you that it's worth it. Because behind that screen you can't let go of, there's a real life waiting for you to come back.

So... **screen OFF, life ON.**

Shall we start?

MY STORY (AND THAT OF MY FAMILY)

I could tell you that, as a psychologist specialized in addictions, I have always been in control. That I am an expert in managing impulses and that, for that reason, I have never been a victim of any dependency. But I would be lying to you.

The truth is, I've been hooked on my cell phone too. And I didn't realize how much until it was too obvious.

It all started innocently enough, as it does for most people. At first, the phone was just a work tool — a convenient way to stay connected with my patients, my family, and the world. But, little by little, it took up more and more space in my daily life: five minutes while waiting in line, ten minutes before going to sleep, a quick glance while I was eating, another while I was watching a series, even when I stopped at every traffic light. Until one day I realized that, without realizing it, my attention was hijacked by a screen.

But the worst thing was not my own addiction. The worst thing was seeing how I had also trapped those I loved the most.

My two children, both teenagers, spent hours and hours locked in their rooms, glued to their cell phones. We talked less and less. I saw them more and more irritable, more distracted, more disconnected from real life. I tried to talk to them, set limits, even impose schedules... but how could I demand that they put down their cell phones if I couldn't do it myself?

And then there was my mother. A woman from another generation, who seemed to have discovered a new world through the screen. What started out as a way to entertain herself ended up becoming her only companion. She spent the day fiddling with her cell phone, jumping from Facebook to WhatsApp, from absurd videos to chain messages that took her nowhere.

One day, during a family dinner, I realized that the three of us — my children, my mother, and I — were sitting together, each of us trapped in our own digital world. No one was talking. No one was making eye contact. We were together, but more alone than ever.

That was my turning point.

From there I decided that, before helping my patients, I had to help myself and my family. I put into practice everything I had learned during years of treatment therapy for other types of addictions, adapted it to digital addiction and experienced it firsthand.

The result of that process is this book. Because I know we are not the only ones. Because I know that you, who are reading this, have probably felt the same as me: trapped, overwhelmed, unable to let go of your cell phone even though you know it is stealing your time and life.

Therefore, here you will not find a discourse from superiority. This book is written from the other side, from the experience of someone who also fell and who, together with his own, learned to get out.

If I could do it, so can you.

And I will be with you every step of the way.

PART ONE

—

AWARENESS RAISING

ARE YOU ADDICTED TO YOUR CELL PHONE? TAKE THE TEST!

Before changing any habit, before starting to build a new lifestyle, there is one thing we must always do: open our eyes.

This first part of the book is not intended to make you change anything yet. Its only objective is to make you aware of the extent to which your cell phone is stealing your time, energy and attention.

You may think that you're no big deal, that you use it "like everyone else", that you have it under control. I don't blame you: most of my patients thought the same before we started — even I did!

But the reality, when we look at it head-on, is often different.

That's why, before we start the 30-day challenge, I want us to do an honesty exercise together. Not to punish you, but to let you know where you are and where you are going to start from.

It doesn't matter if you think you control the use of your cell phone. Today I propose that, for a moment, you be completely honest with yourself and answer this test.

This simple questionnaire will help you detect your level of dependence. Remember: there are no right or wrong answers. Just data that will allow you to make decisions.

Self-assessment test

One of the most common traps of cell phone addiction is self-deception.

Thinking that it's no big deal. That "everyone does it". That it's okay to look at your cell phone for a while longer.

But the reality is that many of the digital habits we consider normal today have a real impact on our well-being, our productivity and our mental health.

For this reason, I have included this simple and quick test.

It will help you to know where you are now, before doing the 30-day challenge.

If you want, you can also share it with family, friends or your own children, so that they also become aware of it.

This test is not a clinical diagnosis.

It is a tool for you to assess and monitor your level of digital dependency.

Answer Yes or No to each question:

	Question	YES	NO
1.	Do you check your cell phone as soon as you get up, even before you get out of bed?		
2.	Is your cell phone the last thing you look at before you go to sleep?		
3.	Do you feel anxious or nervous if you don't know where your cell phone is?		
4.	Do you find it hard to hold a conversation or watch a movie without looking at your cell phone several times?		
5.	Do you often check your cell phone while eating or dining?		
6.	Do you check your cell phone while driving?		
7.	Do you find it difficult to concentrate on a task without being distracted by your cell phone?		
8.	Have you tried to reduce your cell phone usage and failed?		
9.	Do you mind being asked to put down your cell phone when you are with other people?		
10.	Do you compulsively check notifications, even when you know there is nothing important?		
11.	Do you feel like you are wasting your time surfing social networks, but you keep doing it?		
12.	Do you sleep worse or find it difficult to switch off at night because of your cell phone?		
13.	Have you neglected activities, hobbies or people because of your cell phone?		
14.	Do you have the feeling that your day is not going well and suspect that your cell phone has a lot to do with it?		

Results and addiction levels

- **Between 0 and 3 affirmative answers → Controlled use.** Your relationship with your cell phone is relatively healthy. Still, this book will help you reinforce your control and avoid falling into the trap.

- **Between 4 and 7 affirmative answers → Excessive use.** Your cell phone is starting to steal your time, attention and energy. It's time to take action before it goes any further.

- **8 or more affirmative answers → Digital dependence.** Your cell phone is conditioning your life. This book will not only help you, but it is urgent that you start the challenge today.

Remember: This is not a clinical diagnosis, but it is a fairly accurate snapshot of your situation.

Don't beat yourself up if the result worries you. You are here, you have taken the test and that is already your first step to change.

In the next few chapters, I'll show you exactly what your cell phone is doing to your brain, your time and your life. And then, together, we'll start the challenge.

WHAT YOUR CELL PHONE IS DOING TO YOUR BRAIN (AND YOUR LIFE)

You may think I'm exaggerating when I talk about addiction. After all, what harm can a small device that fits in your pocket do you?

I hear you. For years, I too thought it was just a tool, a way to stay informed, to communicate, to entertain myself.

Until I began to see, in my practice and in my own home, the real effects of this "tool".

The cell phone - or rather, the misuse we make of it - **is changing your brain, your mood and the way you live.** And not for the better.

Today I want you to understand what is going on inside you every time you unlock the screen.

What does the cell phone do to your brain?

Let's start with the head. Numerous studies have shown that excessive use of cell phones and social networks causes real changes in the functioning of your brain. Here is a summary of the most important ones:

- **Increased anxiety and stress.**

    Every notification, every message, every "like" generates a small spike in **dopamine**, the pleasure hormone. This creates an immediate reward circuit that your brain constantly seeks out.

    But it also causes anxiety when you don't receive those stimuli, creating a cycle of dependency.

- **Attention deficit.**

   Continuous exposure to notifications, interruptions and digital multitasking reduces your ability to concentrate. You find it increasingly difficult to maintain your attention for long periods of time. Sound familiar?

- **Increased risk of depression.**

   Excessive use of social and mobile networks has been associated with an increased risk of depression, especially in adolescents and young adults. Constant comparison, external validation and hyperconnection directly affect self-esteem and mood.

- **Emotional isolation.**

   Paradoxically, the more digitally connected we are, the more emotionally disconnected we feel. Dependence on screens weakens real relationships and increases the feeling of loneliness.

What does the cell phone do to your sleep?

Another of the most visible (and dangerous) effects is the impact on sleep quality:

- **Blue light from screens alters your circadian rhythm.**

   This bluish light before bed inhibits the production of melatonin, the hormone responsible for regulating sleep, making it harder for you to fall asleep and your sleep more shallow.

- **Mental overstimulation makes it difficult to rest.**

    The cell phone is usually the last thing we look at before going to sleep. Consuming digital content until late keeps your brain in a state of alertness, making it difficult to disconnect and more difficult to fall asleep.

- **Nocturnal awakenings and interrupted sleep.**

    The habit of looking at your cell phone if you wake up at night fragments your sleep and directly affects the quality of your rest.

- **Chronic fatigue and low performance.**

    Excessive use of the cell phone at night causes fatigue, concentration difficulties, irritability and lower intellectual performance the next day.

What about the physical impact?

Although most of the consequences are psychological, cell phone addiction also affects your body:

- **Neck and back pain ("Text Neck").**

    The inclined and maintained posture while looking at the cell phone generates muscular tensions in the neck, back and shoulders.

- **Vision problems.**

    Prolonged use of screens causes eyestrain, blurred vision, dry eyes and, in some cases, frequent headaches.

- **Sedentary lifestyle and metabolic problems.**

    Time spent on cell phones often replaces time spent in physical activity, which encourages a sedentary lifestyle and, in the long term, increases the risk of obesity, type 2 diabetes and cardiovascular disease.

As we have just seen, every time you receive a notification, a like, a message, your brain releases **dopamine**, the neurotransmitter of pleasure and reward. It is the same substance that is activated by alcohol, gambling, sugar or drugs.

But there's a catch: those little doses of dopamine aren't constant or predictable. You don't know when you'll get a message, when someone will comment on your photo or when you'll see a video you like. That uncertainty keeps your brain **on constant alert**, waiting for the next reward. And that's the hook.

You're not hooked on your cell phone. You're hooked on the dopamine it triggers.

In addition, when you use your cell phone compulsively, your brain begins to lose the ability to get bored, to concentrate and to tolerate frustration. The screen becomes an automatic escape route for any uncomfortable emotion: stress, boredom, sadness, anxiety...

Do you feel reflected in any of these sensations?

I have seen patients who have even abandoned their studies, distanced themselves from their friends, and even deteriorated their relationships because of this behavior.

📌 **Real case: Lucia, 32 years old - "I could no longer concentrate".**

Lucia worked as a graphic designer. She came for consultation because, according to her, she had lost the ability to concentrate. Every time she started to work, after a few minutes she ended up looking at her cell phone "without realizing it". She would check Instagram, read messages, go back to work... and so on, over and over again.

When we monitored her habits through apps, we discovered that she was checking her cell phone **more than 100 times a day** *and had stopped reading books, going for walks and enjoying her friends. Her anxiety level was sky high.*

The most serious thing was not the time I spent in front of the screen, but **everything I had stopped living in the meantime.**

Today, after doing the challenge that you are about to start, Lucia has regained her concentration, has taken up her hobbies and, above all, has regained control of her life.

The false sense of connection

One of the biggest traps of mobile addiction is that it makes us feel connected. We believe that, by spending hours on social networks, sending messages or seeing what others are posting, we are close to others. We feel that we are part of something, that we are not missing out on anything.

But that connection is a mirage.

Apps and social networks are designed to simulate closeness, but in reality they foster a superficial, quick relationship without depth. It's not real connection, it's exposure.

We are seeing edited lives, fragmented messages, emotions packed into an emoji.

What used to be a 10-minute call to see how a friend was doing has now been reduced to a "like" or replying to a story. And the more time we spend on that fake connection, the less time we have for the real connection: looking into each other's eyes, talking face-to-face, hugging, really listening, having a beer with a friend.

The cell phone makes us feel accompanied but often leaves us more alone than ever.

🔹 **Real case: Ana, 28 years old - "I had hundreds of friends, but no one to talk to".**

Ana came to the consultation because she felt lonely. She told me that she was talking to people all day long, that she didn't understand why she felt that way. We reviewed her habits and discovered that she spent almost five hours a day on social networks, sending messages, answering stories, participating in chats.

But when I asked him when was the last time, he had met a friend for coffee or a walk, he didn't know what to answer.

I had hundreds of "friends" online but hadn't seen any of them in person in weeks.

As soon as she started reducing her time on her cell phone and spending that time on real encounters, her feeling of loneliness disappeared.

---

21 - AWARENESS RAISING

It is not your fault, but it is your responsibility.

I want you to understand this: the problem is not you. The problem is a system designed so that you can't stop looking. We'll see it in the next chapter, but I'll give you a preview: the apps you use every day are created by experts in human behavior, whose only goal is to keep you hooked for as long as possible.

You are not weak. You are human.

But now that you know, you have the opportunity to change it.

In the next chapter you'll find out how you've been duped, how the business behind your digital dependency works, and why it's so hard to let go of your cell phone.

And then, we will start together the way out of this

THE BIG CON: WHY YOU CAN'T LET GO OF YOUR CELL PHONE

Now that you know what your cell phone is doing to your brain and your life, I want to tell you something that most people don't know (or prefer not to know): **Your addiction isn't an accident, it's a business.**

Nothing that happens when you use your cell phone is innocent. Social networks, messaging apps, games, mobile brands... They're all designed by experts so you can't put them down. And the more time you spend in there, the more they win.

How does the business work?

It's not your well-being that's at stake. It's your attention.

Every minute you spend looking at the screen, watching videos, scrolling posts or replying to messages, someone is making money. You are not the customer. **You are the product.**

The big technology companies make their living by capturing and selling your attention. And to achieve this, they have created a system that mixes the best (or the worst) of psychology, neuroscience and technology.

They keep you hooked through:

- **Constant notifications:** To interrupt you and keep you coming back again and again.

- **Infinite scroll:** You never know when something interesting will appear.

- **Random rewards:** Sometimes you get a "like", a message or a funny video. And that keeps you looking.

23 - AWARENESS RAISING

- **Social comparison:** They make you feel that others have better, more fun, more successful lives... and get you hooked on watching more.

Everything is designed so that you can't stop.

Apps are designed to get you hooked

I will tell you some of the tricks that apps have created to get us to spend hours hooked on them. Do not think that they are the result of chance, these large corporations have psychologists on staff who know very well the human mind and what keys to play to achieve your addiction.

Twitter's "Pull to refresh" (now X)

One of the best known examples is the "swipe down to update" gesture popularized by Twitter.

What seems like an innocent gesture is directly inspired by slot machines: you don't know what content will appear when you upgrade, and that element of uncertainty triggers your reward system, just like when you pull a lever and wait to see if you win or not.

It was deliberately designed to be addictive.

The infinite scroll of Instagram and TikTok

In the past, social networks had an end. You got to the end of the page and, if you wanted more content, you had to consciously decide to load another page.

Today, apps like Instagram, Facebook or TikTok have implemented infinite scroll, which eliminates any natural brake. There is no end, no pause, no time for your brain to say, "I'm done."

It was a calculated technical and psychological decision, precisely so that you don't stop sliding your finger.

WhatsApp notifications and the "double blue tick".

WhatsApp introduced one of the most effective strategies to generate anxiety and dependency: double blue checkmarks. Knowing that someone has read your message and does not respond to you generates a level of social stress that forces you to constantly log in to the application.

The same goes for the "online" or "writing..." status. Little details designed to keep you on your toes, even if you don't want to.

YouTube and Netflix "Autoplay" mode

YouTube implemented years ago the automatic playback of videos: when one ends, another one starts without you having to do anything. Netflix did the same with episodes of their series. This strategy is designed to eliminate friction and prevent you from making a conscious decision to stop. If you do nothing, you will keep watching.

Apple and Android "Time on Screen".

Interestingly, both Apple and Google introduced their time-of-use monitoring tools years after they contributed to this digital epidemic. They did so when criticism of the negative impact of mobile began to affect their public image, but their design is deliberately unrestrictive and easy to bypass.

Why is it so difficult to let go of the cell phone?

Do you understand now why it's so hard to unhook from your cell phone? Because you're not just fighting a device. You're fighting a system designed to make you fail.

But here comes the good news: when you become aware of this deception, you regain power.

That's why I wanted to dedicate this first part of the book to open your eyes. Because you can't change what you don't see. And now that you see it, now that you know how they trap you, it's time to act.

The next chapter will mark the beginning of your real change. Tomorrow we will start **the 30-day challenge**. A simple, progressive and effective plan to get your life back on track, day by day, step by step.

Be prepared. What starts tomorrow can be the beginning of a much freer life.

26 - AWARENESS RAISING

PART TWO

—

THE 30-DAY CHALLENGE

HOW DOES THE PLAN WORK?

Now that you know how your cell phone is affecting your life, and why it's no coincidence that it's so hard for you to let go, it's time to act.

Here begins your challenge. A simple, practical and effective plan so that, in just 30 days, you can become the owner of your time, your attention and your life again.

This plan is designed so that you can do it even if you have a demanding job, children, responsibilities or even if you think you "don't have time". Because the truth is that you don't need extra time: you just need to decide.

What are we going to do for the next 30 days?

Every day you will find:

- A short motivational and direct text.
- A real case of one of my patients or a personal anecdote related to the challenge of the day.
- A specific exercise or action for that day: the challenge of the day.
- A question for you to think about and become aware of.

I won't ask you to make big changes all at once. This plan is designed for you to progress little by little, to build new habits and, above all, to regain control without feeling like you're giving up anything.

What happens if you miss a day?

Nothing. Absolutely nothing. This is not an exam. There will be days when it will be easy for you and others when it will be harder. The important thing is not to get it perfect, but to keep moving forward.

If one day you don't meet the challenge, nothing happens. Come back the next day and continue. The important thing is not to give up.

What do I need to do this challenge?

You only need three things:

1. Your commitment.

2. A notebook, cell phone notes or any place where you can write down your reflections. If you have this book on paper, each day you will find a space to write. If you need more space, at the end of the book you will find some blank pages for your reflections.

3. You want to get your life back.

What will change in you after these 30 days?

What you will discover is not only that you can live with less phone use. You're going to discover that, behind that screen, you were missing out on a lot:

- Real time.
- Mental energy.
- Authentic relationships.
- And, above all, yourself.

So, if you're ready...

We start tomorrow.

WEEK 1 - TAKE CONTROL

DAY 1 - The first step: knowing how much your cell phone controls you

Before changing any habit, we need to know where we are starting from. Today I'm not going to ask you to do anything difficult. Just look reality in the face, without excuses, without filters.

The curious thing about cell phone addiction is that we are often unaware that we have it. It is a silent dependence, socially accepted, disguised as "normality". We all look at our cell phones at every moment, we all answer messages, we all let ourselves get carried away by the infinite scroll... so we convince ourselves that it's no big deal.

But the data doesn't lie. And today we're going to start by looking at that data.

How much of your life are you giving away to your cell phone? The answer may surprise you.

📌 Real case: Pedro, 19 years old - "I only use it for a while".

Pedro came to my office accompanied by his parents. He was 19 years old and had been locked in his room for months, irritable, unmotivated, isolated. They suspected that the problem was the cell phone, but he insisted that "he only used it for a while".

On the first day of therapy we did a very simple exercise: we installed a usage monitoring app.

When, after a week, we reviewed the figures together, Pedro was silent.

He had spent more than 50 hours in seven days glued to the screen. More than two full days of his life, every week, disappeared between social networks, videos and games.

The most shocking thing for him was not the number of hours, but to discover that he did not remember what he had done in all that time. There were no memories, no experiences, no conversations. Just a feeling of emptiness.

That was the first click. The first time he saw his problem clearly.

◎ Today's challenge

Today you don't have to change anything. Just observe.

Download a screen time monitoring app (ActionDash, QualityTime, Quantum, Zario, or whichever you prefer) or check out the Digital Wellness feature on Android or Usage Time on iPhone.

Note how long you used the cell phone yesterday and how many times you unlocked it.

Observe which applications you spend the most time on.

Do not punish yourself. Don't judge yourself.

Just look at the data.

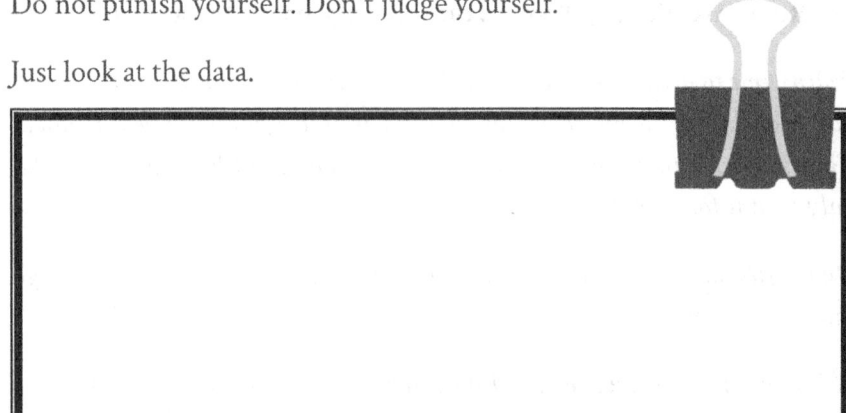

❓ Question for reflection

When you review today's data, ask yourself:

What surprised you more - the total time, the number of unlocks, or the apps you use the most?

DAY 2 - The diary of your addiction

Yesterday you looked at the numbers. Today I want you to look at what doesn't show up in the statistics: your emotions.

Because mobile addiction is not just a matter of time. It has to do with how we feel before, during and after using it. Most of the time we don't pick up the cell phone because we need it. We pick it up because we are uncomfortable, bored, anxious, lonely.

Today I propose that you start listening to what is going on inside you every time you unlock the screen.

📍 **Real case: Marta, 41 years old - "My cell phone was my refuge".**

Marta is a mother of two children and works as an administrative assistant. When she came to the office, she said she felt empty, stressed and did not understand why she spent so many hours in front of her cell phone.

During the first week of therapy, I asked her to keep a digital diary: to write down every time he looked at his cell phone and what he was feeling before he did so.

After a few days, the pattern was clear: every time she had an argument with her partner, every time she felt lonely, every time she had a moment of boredom or sadness... her hand went straight to her cell phone.

The cell phone wasn't the problem. It was the anesthesia.

When Marta realized that she was using the screen to avoid facing her emotions, she began to change. Not because she stopped having those feelings, but because she learned to look at them head on, instead of running away from them.

🎯 Today's challenge

Today I want you to start your digital diary.

Every time you feel the need to look at your cell phone, write it down:

- What were you doing before?
- What were you feeling?
- What were you looking for when you unlocked the screen?

Do it without judging yourself. Just observe. You can use the blank pages at the end of the book.

❔ Question for reflection

When you go through your journal tonight, ask yourself: what emotion comes up most often before you look at your cell phone?

DAY 3 - Detect your triggers

You have already started to observe your habits and emotions. Today we are going to identify the triggers.

A trigger is any situation, emotion or stimulus that prompts you to pick up your cell phone almost without thinking. And they are not always obvious. Sometimes it's boredom. Other times it's discomfort, stress, a silence, a dead moment.

Identifying your triggers is key to changing your relationship with your cell phone. Because if you don't know what leads you to unlock it, you won't be able to stop it.

📌 Case in point: Ed Sheeran and his addiction to social media

Singer Ed Sheeran spoke publicly about his addiction to social networks. For years, he compulsively checked his notifications, his comments, his messages. Every criticism or every compliment was a trigger that led him to spend hours glued to the screen, seeking approval and distraction.

When he recognized that her emotional well-being depended on what others were saying online, he made a radical decision: he shut down his social networks for more than a year.

In his own words, "I was missing out on my life by looking at other people's lives."

Identifying your triggers was the first step in regaining peace of mind.

🎯 Today's challenge

Today I want you to do two things:

1. Review your digital diary from yesterday and underline the situations that are repeated.
2. Make a list of your triggers. What makes you pick up your cell phone? What emotions or situations trigger that impulse?

❓ Question for reflection

What could you do differently the next time one of these triggers appears?

DAY 4 - The notification trap

Today we are going to talk about the most obvious, but also the most powerful trap: **notifications**.

Every sound, vibration or little red number on the screen is a wake-up call. A constant reminder that someone "needs" you, that something is going on, that you "should" look.

But what if I told you that 90% of these notifications are not important, would you agree with me?

What they do is not inform you. What they do is interrupt you, distract you, take away your control.

Every notification is a thief of your attention

🔖 Personal Case: My mother and infinite notifications

My mother, who is over 70 years old, discovered the digital world late, but when she did, she fell head over heels. For a while, every time I visited her, her cell phone wouldn't stop ringing: WhatsApp chains, Facebook alerts, pharmacy notifications, news alerts, promotions... It was impossible to have a conversation without her cell phone interrupting every two minutes.

One day, over coffee, I asked her to count how many notifications she had received in an hour. It was more than 20. She herself realized that her head was everywhere but there, at that table, with me.

I suggested a simple exercise: turn off all notifications other than important calls and messages. The next day she called me and said, "I had a quiet day today, the kind of day I haven't had in a long time."

Sometimes, peace begins by silencing a beep

🎯 Today's challenge

Today you are going to do digital cleaning:

- Deactivate all notifications that are not essential: social networks, offers, games, newsletters...

- Keep only those that are really necessary.

TIP: I find the "Do not disturb" option very useful. You can define which applications can skip it. For example, when I need to concentrate or when I sleep, I activate it and only incoming calls from certain contacts that I consider important ring.

❓ Question for reflection

How do you feel when your cell phone stops interrupting you constantly? What mental space have you gained?

DAY 5 - The multitasking trap

Today we're going to talk about a silent enemy that goes hand in hand with your mobile addiction: **multitasking**.

We live in the age of interruptions. We have been sold the idea that we can do a thousand things at once: answer a message while eating or driving, look at Instagram while watching a series, answer an email while chatting with someone. And we've bought into it.

But the reality is that digital multitasking doesn't exist. Your brain doesn't multitask. What it does is jump from one task to another, over and over again, draining your energy and reducing your ability to concentrate. And the cell phone is the main culprit of this constant jumping.

Every time you interrupt what you're doing to look at your cell phone, even if it's just for a second, your brain needs time to refocus. And if you add up those little interruptions throughout the day, the result is devastating: mental exhaustion, feelings of dissatisfaction, difficulty concentrating, anxiety.

📌 **Real case: Javier, 27 years old - "I couldn't finish anything"**.

Javier works as a programmer. When he came to the office, he complained that he had lost the ability to concentrate. The funny thing is that he was convinced that he was "very productive", because he was always doing several things at the same time: answering messages, checking networks, working and answering emails, all at the same time.

But when we analyzed his routine together, we discovered that this supposed productivity was a mirage. Javier took twice as long to finish any task. His anxiety was sky high. He didn't sleep well. And worst of all, he felt that he didn't enjoy anything, that everything was happening too fast.

The day he turned off notifications and started working with his cell phone away from his desk, he wrote me a message, "I've been at it for two days and I can already feel the difference. I didn't remember what it was like to do one thing and enjoy it."

🎯 Today's challenge

Today I propose a simple but powerful exercise:

- For the next 24 hours, when you do any activity - working, eating, reading, talking to someone, watching a series - leave your cell phone away.

- No looking at the screen while doing something else.

- If you find it difficult, observe what you feel: anxiety, boredom, discomfort... Write it down in your diary.

❓ Question for reflection

How does your experience change when you do only one thing at a time? What does it feel like to be present?

DAY 6 - Digital Silence: Learn to be without noise

We live surrounded by noise. But not only sound noise (traffic, people talking, construction sites, appliances...). Today I want you to think about **digital noise**.

We are so used to receiving information, stimuli, images, videos, messages, that when there is a moment of silence - an elevator, a queue, a traffic light - we immediately fill it with our cell phones. We no longer know how to be alone with our thoughts.

The cell phone has stolen our silence. And with it, it has stolen our calm.

What we don't know is that the silence we avoid is precisely what we need to rest, to connect with ourselves, to put our ideas in order.

📌 Case Study: Simon Sinek and digital noise

Simon Sinek, speaker and author of leadership books, has spoken in many interviews about how technology has invaded every part of our lives. He himself confessed that for years he could not spend five minutes waiting in a restaurant without looking at his cell phone.

One day he decided to try something different: leave his cell phone at home when he went for a walk.

The first day was uncomfortable, almost unbearable. But after a few days, he discovered that in those moments of silence his best ideas, his most valuable reflections, began to emerge.

Today he defends the importance of seeking screen-free spaces to recover deep thinking.

🎯 Today's challenge

You're probably already imagining it. Today, I want you to seek at least 30 minutes of digital silence.

- Go for a walk without a cell phone.
- If you are at home, leave your cell phone in another room.
- Allow yourself to be bored, to think, to listen to the silence.

? Question for reflection

What have you discovered in those 30 minutes of silence? What feeling do you have when you finish?

DAY 7 - First reflection: What are you recovering?

You have reached the end of the first week - congratulations!

You may not have realized it, but these first few days you have already begun to regain something you thought you had lost: control.

You've started to observe your habits, become aware of your triggers, reduce notifications, avoid multitasking and seek moments of silence.

That is no small thing. It is the beginning of a very profound change.

Today I am not going to propose any new challenge. Today I just want you to look back and reflect on what has happened in these seven days.

📌 Personal case: My children and the first week

I remember when I started this same challenge with my children. At first, like many teenagers, they complained, protested, made excuses. But after the first week, something happened that I did not expect: one afternoon, while we were having coffee, Carlos, my eldest son said to me:

"Mom, the other day I went an hour without looking at my cell phone...and it was weird, but it was also quiet. Before, I didn't even realize what I was doing all day."

That was the first click. The beginning of a change that, little by little, transformed his relationship with technology.

🎯 Today's challenge

Today I want you to calmly answer these questions:

1. What have you learned about yourself this week?

2. What habit has been the most difficult for you to change?

3. What small victory have you achieved?

4. How do you feel when you spend some time without your cell phone?

Write down your answers. We will need them later.

Summary - Week 1: Take control

You have reached the end of the first week of this challenge. And although right now it may seem to you that you haven't made any major changes, believe me: you have set in motion the most important transformation. This first week was not meant to make you give up your cell phone, nor was it meant to make you change your habits all at once. Its only goal was to open your eyes.

And you have succeeded.

Here is a summary of the steps you have taken:

- **Day 1:** You figured out how much of your life you are giving away to your cell phone. You measured and looked at the data head on, no excuses.

- **Day 2:** You opened a digital diary to understand what you were looking for every time you unlocked your cell phone.

- **Day 3:** You identified your triggers. Those moments, emotions or routines that push you to look at your cell phone.

- **Day 4:** You cleaned up notifications that were constantly interrupting you and hijacking your attention.

- **Day 5:** You discovered the real impact of multitasking and started testing what happens when you do only one thing at a time.

- **Day 6:** You recovered the value of silence, allowing you to be without digital stimuli for a while.

- **Day 7:** You made a first reflection on everything you had already achieved and learned.

This week you have started to take control. You've stopped living on autopilot and started to be aware of how, when and why you use your cell phone. **That's already a big step**

WEEK 2 - CUT THE CHAINS

If in the first week you opened your eyes, this week it's time to start cutting the cords that tie you to your cell phone.

You know how much time you spend glued to your screen, you've identified your triggers and you've cleared the notifications that kept you on constant alert. Now it's time to take real action. To start detaching, even if it's little by little.

I'm not going to ask you to throw your cell phone out the window. It's not about giving up technology. It's about taking back control.

Get ready. This week we start cutting chains.

DAY 8 - Eliminate Toxic Apps

Have you ever opened an app without knowing why? Have you logged in "just for a minute" and realized, an hour later, that you're still there?

That's no accident. There are apps designed to grab your attention and not let you leave. Social networks, games, sensationalist news apps...

Not all applications are equal. Some add up. Others simply steal your time and energy.

Today we are going to do some cleaning.

📌 **Real case: Raul, 34 years old - "I couldn't stop looking".**

Raul works as a salesman and spends many hours alone, traveling. He told me he was "killing time" on social networks. But when we checked his cell phone together, we saw that he had installed 27 applications that he consulted every day, compulsively: Instagram, TikTok, Twitter, forums, games.... The most surprising thing was that, when I asked him what he remembered of everything he had seen on those apps the previous week, he couldn't tell me anything.

We started with a simple exercise: uninstalling three applications that did not contribute anything and consumed most of his time. At first it was hard for him. After a week, he told me:

"Now, when I get bored, I read a book. It's been years since I've done that."

🎯 Today's challenge

Today I want you to do some digital cleaning:

- Check your mobile and delete at least 3 apps that you know waste your time and do not contribute anything to you.

- If you are reluctant to delete them, at least hide or deactivate them during this week.

❓ Question for reflection

How does it feel to delete those apps? What mental or emotional space have you freed up?

DAY 9 - Clean your screen: less is more

Your home screen is a mirror of your mind.

The more apps, icons, notifications and shortcuts you have in sight, the more scattered your attention will be. It's like having a desk full of papers, post-its, books and useless objects: it's impossible to concentrate.

Today we are going to make digital order. Because the clutter in your phone is a reflection of the clutter in your head.

📌 Personal case: My own experiment

For years, my home screen was full of icons: social networks, news, games, emails, online stores... Every time I unlocked my phone, my mind jumped from one stimulus to another, even when I didn't need to use any of those apps.

One day I decided to try something: I left only the essential applications (phone, messages, calendar, notes) and hid the rest.

The first day I felt lost. The second, I started to notice that I was unlocking my phone less. After a week, I realized that I had stopped logging into social networks on impulse.

Sometimes, the first step to peace of mind is to clean up the digital space around you.

🎯 Today's challenge

- Tidy up your home screen.
- Leave only the essential apps.
- The rest, move them to another folder or secondary screen so that they are not always in view.

❓ Question for reflection

How do you feel when your cell phone is clean and tidy? How many fewer times have you unlocked the screen today?

DAY 10 - Put a price on your time

Today I want you to think about something very important: how much is your time worth?

Every minute you spend looking at your cell phone has a cost. A cost in time, in attention, in well-being, in relationships, in opportunities.

If you add up the hours you spend on your cell phone every week, you'll see that you're giving away the equivalent of a whole day of your life.
In exchange for what? a few videos? a few "likes"? killing time?

Today I want you to put a price on your time. Because only when you realize what you are giving away, you start to value what you are losing.

📌 Case in point: Bill Gates and the weather

Bill Gates, one of the busiest men in the world, has a habit known as "Think Weeks": once or twice a year, he isolates himself for a whole week with no cell phone, no mail, no meetings, to read, think and reflect.

Why? Because he understands that his time and attention are the most valuable resource he has. He knows that every hour he spends distracted is an hour he will never get back.

Gates claims that these weeks are the most productive and creative weeks of his year. Not because of everything he does, but because of everything he doesn't do. You don't need to be a billionaire to value your time. You just need to be aware of how much it's worth to you.

🎯 Today's challenge

- Calculate how many hours you have spent on your mobile this week (you can look at the data in Digital Wellbeing or Usage Time or in the apps you downloaded on the first day).

- Multiply those hours by what you would earn in your hourly job, or by the value you would place on your free time. If you don't work or don't know how much an hour of your time might be worth, you can take an approximate value, for example, 15 euros per hour.

- Write down how much your cell phone addiction "cost" you this week.

? Question for reflection

What could you have done this week with those hours you gave away to the screen? What could you have bought with that money?

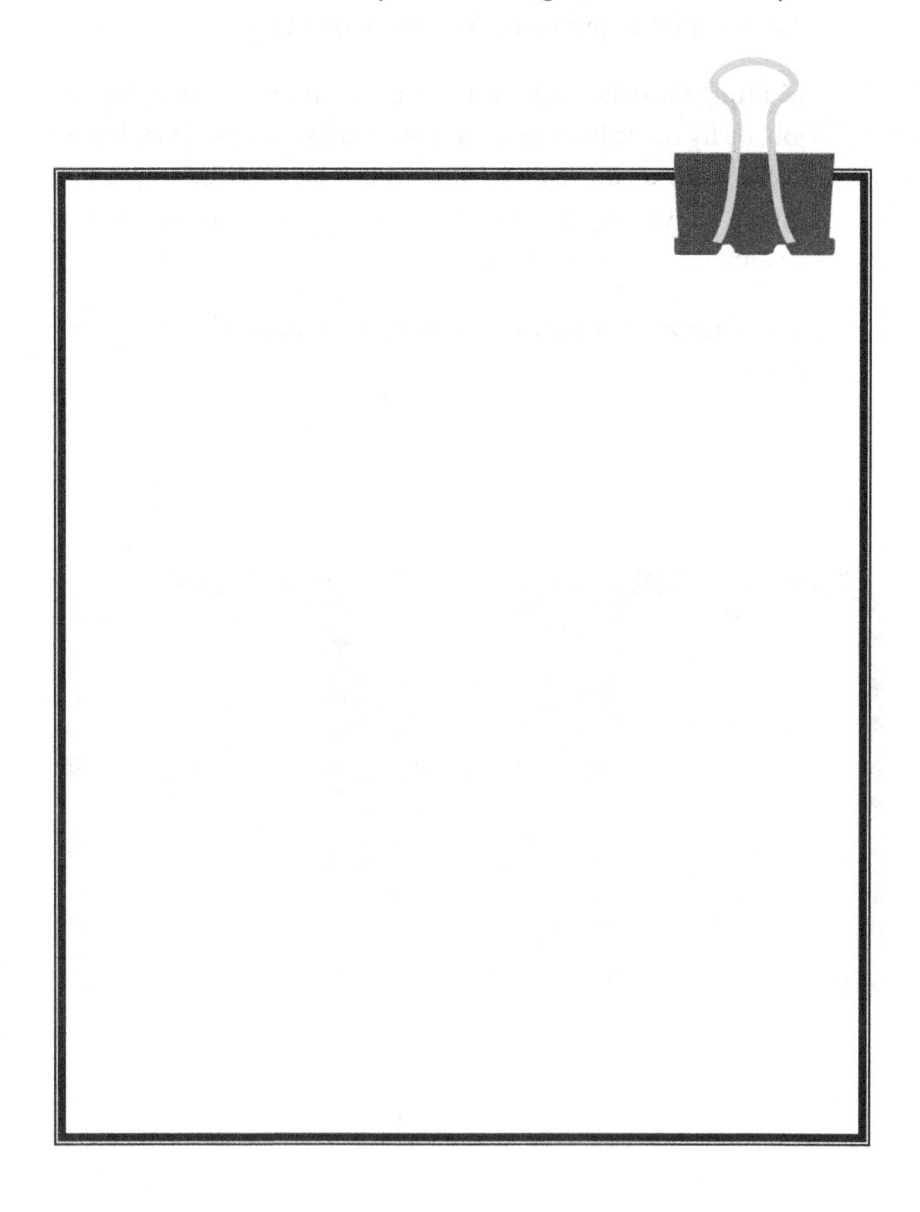

DAY 11 - Create mobile-free zones

Today we are going to start setting physical limits.

Your relationship with your cell phone depends not only on your willpower. It also depends on where your cell phone is and how it conditions the spaces you inhabit. If your cell phone is always within reach - in bed, on the table, in the bathroom - it is practically impossible to resist the temptation to look at it.

That's why today we are going to create mobile-free zones. Places where, as a rule, your cell phone cannot enter. Spaces for you, for the people around you, to rest, to disconnect.

Because it's not enough to want to use it less. You need to build an environment that helps you achieve it.

📌 **Real case: Elena, 39 years old - "We couldn't have dinner without our cell phone".**

Elena came to the consultation exhausted. She told me that she did not understand why her children did not talk to her, why there was so much silence at home.

When we started talking, we discovered that, during dinners, each of them - she, her husband and her two children - had their cell phones on the table. At first it was "to see a notification", "in case there was something urgent", "out of habit"... but the reality was that they had stopped talking to each other.

I proposed a simple exercise: to create a cell phone-free zone at the table. During lunches and dinners, all cell phones were left in another room.

On the first day, there were complaints. The second day, uncomfortable glances. A week later, the conversations returned.

Sometimes, just creating the space is enough to make the real connection happen.

🎯 Today's challenge

- Choose two areas of your home that, starting today, will be mobile-free (for example: the dining table and the bedroom).

- Meet this standard without excuses.

❓ Question for reflection

What changes in your home or in your routine when the cell phone is not present in those spaces?

DAY 12 - Redefine your downtime

Many of the times we pick up our cell phones are not because we need them, but because we don't know what to do with the time.

Waiting in line at the supermarket, in the elevator, on the bus, at a traffic light, while waiting for the Netflix movie to load, before going to sleep....

Those "dead" moments that we used to occupy looking around, thinking or simply resting, we now fill compulsively with the screen.

Today we are going to recover those little gaps. Because, believe it or not, that's where the best ideas happen, the important thoughts, the reflections that never come because your cell phone doesn't leave you space for them.

Have you ever come up with a solution to a problem or a good idea while taking a shower? Indeed, when you're not looking at your cell phone.

◆ Case History: Albert Einstein and boredom

Not everyone knows that Einstein had the habit of staring into the void for hours, thinking, without distractions.

Today, many psychologists agree that these spaces of apparent inactivity are key to creativity, reflection and emotional well-being.

In our time, we have lost those spaces because, as soon as we have a free minute, we pick up our cell phones. And without realizing it, we have run out of time to think.

🎯 Today's challenge

- During today's day, when you have "down time" (waiting, in public transportation, waiting in line), do not use your cell phone.

- Observe, think, look around you, listen to your own thoughts.

❓ Question for reflection

What did you discover today when you allowed yourself to be bored? How did it make you feel?

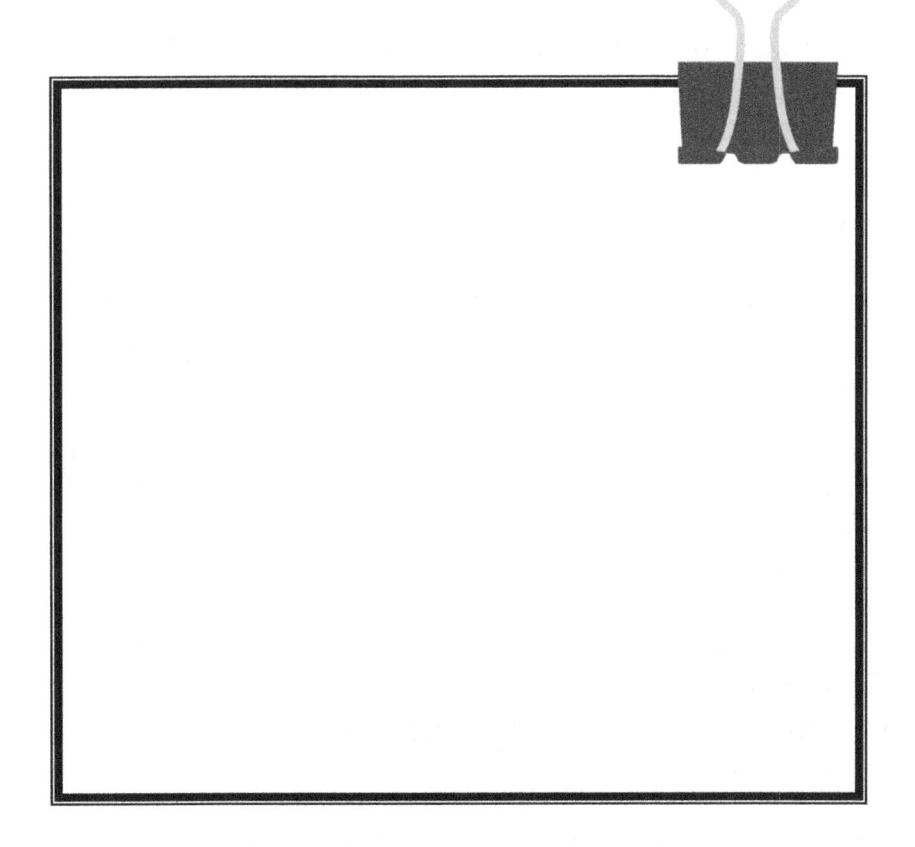

DAY 13 - Recovering a lost hobby

One of the greatest silent tragedies of cell phone addiction is all the things we have stopped doing.

Before the screen took up every hole in your life, what things did you like to do? Maybe you liked reading, cooking, drawing, playing a game, learning a language, playing an instrument, going for a walk?

But little by little, those hobbies were pushed to the back burner. Not because you no longer liked them, but because the cell phone took their place.

Today I want you to start getting back one of those little things that used to make you happy.

♦ Real case: Victor, 52 years old - "I stopped playing guitar".

Victor is a teacher and amateur guitarist. For years, after work, he spent an hour a day playing the guitar. But one day he stopped, without knowing why.

When he came to the clinic, he spoke of tiredness, stress, and a feeling of emptiness. When we reviewed his habits together, we discovered that that hour a day had been replaced, almost without realizing it, by social networks, videos and endless scrolling.

I set him a challenge: every time he was tempted to pick up his cell phone when he got home, he should pick up his guitar. Within a month, he had not only regained his hobby. His anxiety had diminished and his mood had improved markedly.

Sometimes, your phone doesn't just steal your time — it steals a part of who you are.

🎯 Today's challenge

- Today, choose a hobby or activity that you enjoyed before you spent so much time on your cell phone.

- Dedicate at least 30 minutes to take it up again.

❓ Question for reflection

How did it feel to go back to doing something you had put aside? What would you like to recover from now on?

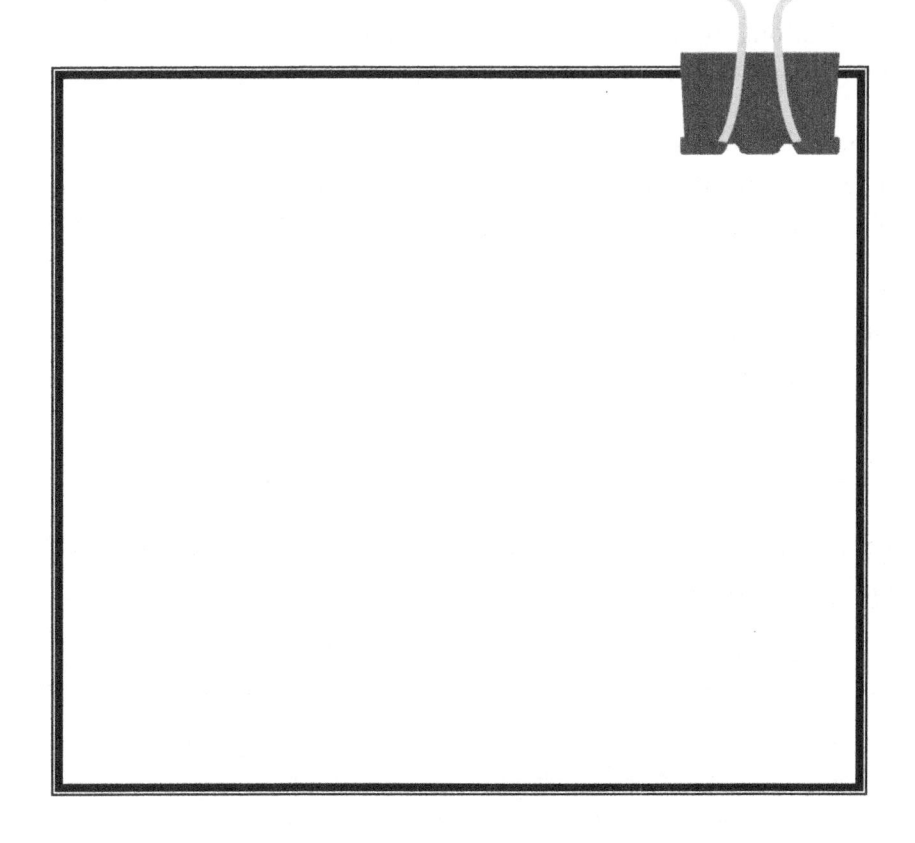

DAY 14 - Second reflection: What do you feel when you turn off the screen?

Today you close the second week of this challenge. And I want you to stop for a moment. To look back and be aware of all that you have already achieved.

You may not have realized it, but in just two weeks you have begun to transform your relationship with your cell phone. You have become aware of how much time it controls you, you have identified the triggers that lead you to use it without thinking, you have cleaned notifications, tidied up your screen, created mobile-free zones and started to recover habits and hobbies that you had forgotten.

I know that some days you may have struggled. I know that others you may have felt anxiety, emptiness, boredom. And I also know that, even if only at times, you have begun to feel a bit of freedom.

Today I want you to stop and reflect. Not to judge you, but to become aware of the road you have already traveled.

◆ Personal Case: My son and the day he turned off the screen

I remember a specific day, in the second week of this same challenge that I did with my children.

My youngest son, after dinner, got up, left his cell phone in another room and sat down to read a book. Without anyone asking him to. When I asked him why, he said, "I noticed today that every time I put my cell phone down, I'm calmer." That day I knew the change had begun. Not because he had stopped using his cell phone completely, but because he had regained the ability to decide.

That is the goal of this challenge. Not that you live without a cell phone, but that you can turn it off whenever you want.

🎯 Today's challenge

Today I want you to take a few minutes to answer these questions:

- What has changed in you since you started the challenge?
- Which habit has cost you the most?
- What habit has surprised you by how easy or how beneficial it has been?
- How do you feel when you spend some time without your cell phone?

Write down your answers. They will be useful for next week.

Week 2 Summary: Cut the chains

You've done a lot more this week than you realize. Here is a summary of the challenges you have overcome:

- **Day 8:** You eliminated toxic apps that only stole your time and attention.
- **Day 9:** Cleaned and tidied your screen to reduce temptation.
- **Day 10:** You calculated the real price you are paying for your time in front of your cell phone.
- **Day 11:** You created mobile-free zones in your home, recovering spaces for you and yours.
- **Day 12:** You rediscovered your downtime, learning not to always fill it with the screen.
- **Day 13:** You recovered a hobby or activity that you had put aside because of your cell phone.
- **Day 14:** You have taken stock and become aware of all the progress you have already made.

This week has not been easy. But you have started to cut the chains

And next week, we're going to go even further: you'll learn how to replace the habit and reconnect with real life.

WEEK 3 - REPLACE THE HABIT

You're halfway there. You've opened your eyes, identified the cell phone traps, cut some visible chains and started to regain control.

But there's one thing I want you to understand: it's not enough to eliminate a habit. **You have to replace it.**

Because if you just remove the cell phone, there will be a void. And if you don't fill that void, inertia will drag you back to the screen.

For years, the cell phone has occupied your downtime, your moments of boredom, your breaks between activities. It has been your refuge when you didn't know what to do with yourself.

In this third week, we are going to fill that void. We are going to replace the habit of looking at the cell phone with the habit of living. Of being present. Of enjoying things you've forgotten about.

Don't expect this week to be easy. You're likely to feel a little "digital monkey". That, not having the screen, you will feel restless, uncomfortable.

That's normal. That means you're breaking an addiction and getting back something much more valuable: your time and attention.

This week will teach you to reconnect with the real world and yourself. We're going to plant new habits, not to forbid you anything, but for you to discover that, when the cell phone disappears, life goes on - and it's much better than you remembered.

DAY 15 - Rediscover boredom

Today begins the third week of the challenge. And we're going to start with something that may make you uncomfortable, but it's fundamental: you're going to learn how to get bored.

I know it sounds strange, but who wants to be bored in a world that offers us constant stimuli?

But boredom is not your enemy. Boredom is the space where creativity, ideas and true zest for life reappear. For years, your cell phone has protected you from boredom. Whenever there was a gap, a silence, a moment of waiting... there was the screen, filling the void.

But that vacuum was not a bad thing. It was necessary.

Why do we fear boredom?

Because it forces us to be with ourselves. Because it confronts us with emotions, thoughts and sensations that we usually avoid.

But when you learn to endure boredom, you become strong. You regain the ability to observe, to create, to decide what you want to do with your time.

Boredom is uncomfortable, yes, but it is also a space of freedom.

📌 **Case in point: Steve Jobs and his undistracted walks.**

Steve Jobs, founder of Apple, had the habit of taking long walks without any kind of stimulus. No music, no cell phone (when smartphones did not yet exist), no company.

He himself said that his best ideas, the most brilliant solutions, came on those walks, when he allowed his mind to wander without distractions.

I'll tell you a secret: I've been walking without a cell phone for years, and the idea of writing this book came up during one of those walks.

Today's challenge

Today, find a time of the day to do nothing for at least 30 minutes. No cell phone, no TV, no music. Just you, your thoughts and silence. Be bored.

If you find it difficult, start with 10 or 15 minutes and increase gradually. Observe what happens inside you when there are no external stimuli. What thoughts appear. What sensations arise.

It may be uncomfortable at first. But, if you persevere, you will discover that this empty space is more valuable than you imagined.

Question for reflection

What have you felt when you allowed yourself to be bored? What discoveries have you made when you weren't filling the void with the screen?

DAY 16 - Learn not to respond right away.

Today we are going to work on one of the most invisible -and most harmful- behaviors generated by cell phone addiction: **the obligation to always respond** immediately to everything.

We live in a world that rewards immediacy. It seems that if you don't answer a message instantly, you are failing. If you don't answer an email in five minutes, you're not efficient. If you don't react to every notification, you're falling behind.

But the reality is different: every time you respond immediately, you are not making a decision. You are reacting. You are giving away your time and attention to others.

Today I want you to start taking back the power to decide when and how you respond. Because that is where true freedom lies.

📌 Real case: Luis, 37 years old - "I lived by WhatsApp".

Luis works as a salesman and is the father of two young children. When he arrived at the office, he told me: "I don't have a minute to myself. All day long answering messages, emails, calls. And if I don't answer quickly, I feel like I let everyone down."

During the challenge, when we reached this point, I proposed an exercise that at first seemed impossible to him: not to answer any message for the next 30 minutes after receiving it, except for real emergencies.

The first day he had a hard time. He felt anxious, like I was failing someone. But little by little, something changed. He told me, "I have discovered that 90% of the messages I answer were not urgent. And that by the time I wait, most of the problems have already resolved themselves."

What Luis understood was something essential: responding immediately is not synonymous with efficiency. Responding immediately means that you are not managing your time. You are letting others manage it for you.

Regain control of your attention

Every time you react to a message, a notification, a call, you are interrupting what you were doing. You're letting others direct your attention. You are fragmenting your day into a thousand pieces of distraction.

Today you are going to start breaking that pattern.

It's not about ignoring the people you love or putting your work aside. It's about regaining your ability to decide when and how you want to respond.

🎯 Today's challenge

For the next 24 hours, apply this rule: Every time you receive a message, mail or notification, wait at least 30 minutes before responding.

If the message is really urgent (few are), you will be able to reply sooner. But most of the time, you'll find that you can wait. That nothing is wrong. That the world keeps on turning.

Observe what emotions appear when doing so: anxiety, discomfort, relief?

❓ Question for reflection

At the end of the day, write down or reflect:

How many times have you broken the rule?

What did it feel like to wait before responding?

What has changed in your day by not reacting instantly?

DAY 17 - Conscious movement without distractions

Today I propose something different: It's not about reading, or meditating, or talking. It is about moving. But to move with attention.

We live in our heads. We jump from screen to screen, from message to message, from thought to thought. And in this digital chaos, we lose something essential: the connection with our body.

Today I want you to start regaining that connection. You don't need to play sports or go to the gym. You just have to move... and be present.

Why move without distractions?

Because your body stores tension, stress, restlessness. And the screen doesn't let you feel it. When you move with attention, you begin to release, to unload, to reconnect. In addition, moving with awareness reinforces what we are working on: being present.

🔸 Real case: Nuria, 40 years old - "I hadn't felt in my body for years".

Nuria is an administrative assistant, mother, and led a sedentary and digital life. When she started this challenge, she felt scattered, nervous, disconnected from herself.

I proposed something very simple: play a soft song, close your eyes and move slowly for 10 minutes. Without thinking. Just feeling.

A few days later, she told me, "I felt weird at first, like I was out of place. But then I started noticing parts of my body I didn't even remember. I felt like I was back inside myself." That small act of presence changed the way she lived day to day.

🎯 Today's challenge

Today, I want you to choose one of these options and do it without a cell phone, without music, without distractions:

- Walk slowly for 15 minutes paying attention to your breathing and each step.
- Do a short conscious stretching routine (10 minutes is enough).
- Dance to a song without looking at your cell phone, without recording yourself, without thinking about how you do it.
- Try a yoga sequence or slow movements (you can look for a guided video but then turn off your cell phone).

As you do this, observe: How does your body feel today? Where is there tension? Where is there calm? What happens when you move without thinking about anything else?

❓ Question for reflection

What did you feel today as you moved without distractions? What parts of you did you rediscover as you paid attention to your body?

DAY 18 - Recover the real conversation

Today we are going to work on something that mobile addiction has silently deteriorated: real conversation, face to face, without digital interruptions.

You may not realize it, but when your cell phone takes center stage, conversations change. You no longer listen the same way. You no longer look into your eyes. You are no longer truly present.

And when you lose the ability to converse, you lose the ability to connect.

Today I want you to recover that essential space: the one of shared words without screens in between.

When someone speaks to you and you are present, you are not just listening.
You're saying, without words, **"I'm here. I care about you. Your story deserves my attention."**

That doesn't make it an emoji. A "like" doesn't do it. Your real presence does.

📌 **Real case: Carlos, 28 years old - "I realized that I was no longer listening".**

Carlos is a bright young man, sociable, always connected. When he came to the office, he told me that he had the feeling that his relationships were superficial, that his friends didn't tell him important things.

When we analyzed his habits, we discovered that, during any conversation, Carlos couldn't help but look at his cell phone every few minutes. While his partner was talking, while he was having dinner with friends, while he was with his family... there was always a notification, a quick glance, a distraction.

When he came to the office, it wasn't for phone addiction — but while he was explaining his case to me, he could not help but consult his cell phone several times while I was talking to him. I set him a simple and tough challenge: have a conversation for at least 30 minutes with someone, without looking at his cell phone once.

The first time, Carlos told me he felt anxious. But he also told me something that marked me: "I realized that I wasn't listening. That my head had been somewhere else for years when someone was talking to me. And that night, when I was finally present, my partner told me things he had never told me."

That day, Carlos recovered the real conversation. And you're going to do it today.

🎯 **Today's challenge**

Today, look for someone important to you: your partner, a friend, a family member, a co-worker. Make it a point to have a 30-minute conversation without a cell phone. Leave your cell phone far away, in another room if possible.

Really listen. Ask questions. Look them in the eye. Don't interrupt. See what happens when you are fully present.

When finished, reflect:

1. How has the conversation changed by not having the cell phone in front of you?

2. What have you discovered about that person that you hadn't noticed before?

❓ Question for reflection

How long has it been since you've had a long, real conversation without digital interruptions? What did you get back today by doing so?

DAY 19 - Regain your focus

Today we are going to work on one of the most devastating effects of digital addiction: the loss of mindfulness.

Maybe you hadn't noticed, but the cell phone not only steals your time. It also fragments your mind. We have become accustomed to living with divided attention, always waiting for a notification, a message, a stimulus. The sadly famous multitasking. And that comes at a price: we no longer know how to be in one place, at one time, with all five senses.

Today I want you to retrain your ability to be present. And for that, we are going to do something very simple and very powerful: go for a walk without your cell phone.

It's not about exercise. It's not about meeting a challenge. It's about being present again.

When you walk without a cell phone, your mind becomes orderly. Your thoughts calm down. Your attention returns to the moment.

And you begin to notice what you had stopped seeing.

🔖 **Case in point: Haruki Murakami and the power of undistracted movement.**

Haruki Murakami is not only one of the most widely read and admired novelists in the world. He is also an example of discipline, presence and mind-body connection in a world saturated with stimuli.

In his book "What I talk about when I talk about running", Murakami shares how, for decades, he has maintained a daily routine of running outdoors, with no distractions, no music, no cell phone. Just him, his body, his breathing and the rhythm of his thoughts.

Murakami started running when he quit his job at a jazz bar to become a writer. He understood that, to write with clarity and depth, he needed physical and mental balance. And he discovered that he found that balance by running. Not running to compete. Running to listen to the silence, empty his mind and reconnect with himself.

He says so himself in his book: "Running every day allows me to maintain my physical fitness, but also my mental fitness. While I run, my thoughts get in order. Worries drift away. And, in that space, ideas emerge."

Murakami doesn't talk about the cell phone, because his habit began long before the digital age. But his message is more valid than ever: in a world that drags us outward, toward the urgent, toward the superficial, the body can be the anchor that brings us back to the present.

Walking or running without a cell phone, without headphones, without distractions, is today an act of resistance. And also a door to find yourself again.

🎯 Today's challenge

- Today, set aside at least 30 minutes to go for a walk without your cell phone
- Choose a place you like: a park, your neighborhood, the beach, the city.
- Leave your cell phone at home or turn it off and store it out of reach.

- As you walk, pay attention to everything: the sounds, the smells, the people, the sky, your breath.

When you finish, write down or reflect:

1. What have you felt when walking without distractions?
2. What details had you been missing?
3. How has it been different from other mobile walks?

```
┌─────────────────────────────────────┐
│                                     │
│                                     │
│                                     │
│                                     │
└─────────────────────────────────────┘
```

? Question for reflection

What did you rediscover today as you walked without a screen? How did it make you feel to be, at last, alone with yourself and the world?

```
┌─────────────────────────────────────┐
│                                     │
│                                     │
│                                     │
│                                     │
└─────────────────────────────────────┘
```

DAY 20 - What emotion are you avoiding with your cell phone?

There are times when you unlock your phone without thinking about it. You feel uncomfortable, nervous, bored, sad... and without realizing it, you are already inside an app. You're not looking for anything specific. You're just looking to escape.

And the fact is that the cell phone is often not just a distraction. It is an emotional escape route.

We have become accustomed to avoid feeling. And the cell phone has become an immediate anesthetic for everything we don't want to face: boredom, anxiety, loneliness, tiredness, uncertainty, sadness.

But the truth is this: Until you learn to feel without running away, you will remain a slave to the impulse to look at a screen.

It's not about getting rid of your cell phone. It's about learning to stop before you use it as a refuge. About learning to ask yourself, "What emotion is here that I don't want to feel?"

And little by little, without demands, you begin to practice the courage to be with yourself... without screens.

📌 **Real case: Ana, 35 years old - "Whenever I felt lonely, I picked up my cell phone".**

At the time she came to the office, Ana was working from home. She had a partner, friends, a seemingly stable life. But when she started this challenge, she told me: "I can't stand moments of silence. When I'm alone, the first thing I do is look at my cell phone. I don't care what's there. I just need to not think."

During her third week, we focused on observing that impulse. Every time she felt the urge to look at her cell phone for no clear reason, she had to stop and ask herself, "What am I feeling right now?"

At first, she felt exposed. Vulnerable. She told me she realized she used her cell phone to avoid feeling lonely. But gradually she began to hold on to that feeling. To not run away. To breathe. To be with herself.

"For the first time in years," she told me, "I didn't feel like loneliness was something I had to cover up. It was just part of me. And there was nothing wrong. There was nothing wrong with being alone."

⊙ Today's challenge

During today, every time you feel the urge to look at your cell phone for no clear reason, stop and ask yourself:

- What am I feeling right now?
- Am I using my cell phone so I don't feel this?
- Can I sustain this emotion without escaping?

On at least two of those occasions, choose **not to look at your cell phone**. Instead, breathe deeply for 1 minute. Notice your body. Accept the emotion that comes up. Don't run away.

? Question for reflection

At the end of the day, reflect:

1. What emotions do you usually cover up with your cell phone?

2. What has it been like to hold them without a screen?

3. What have you discovered about yourself?

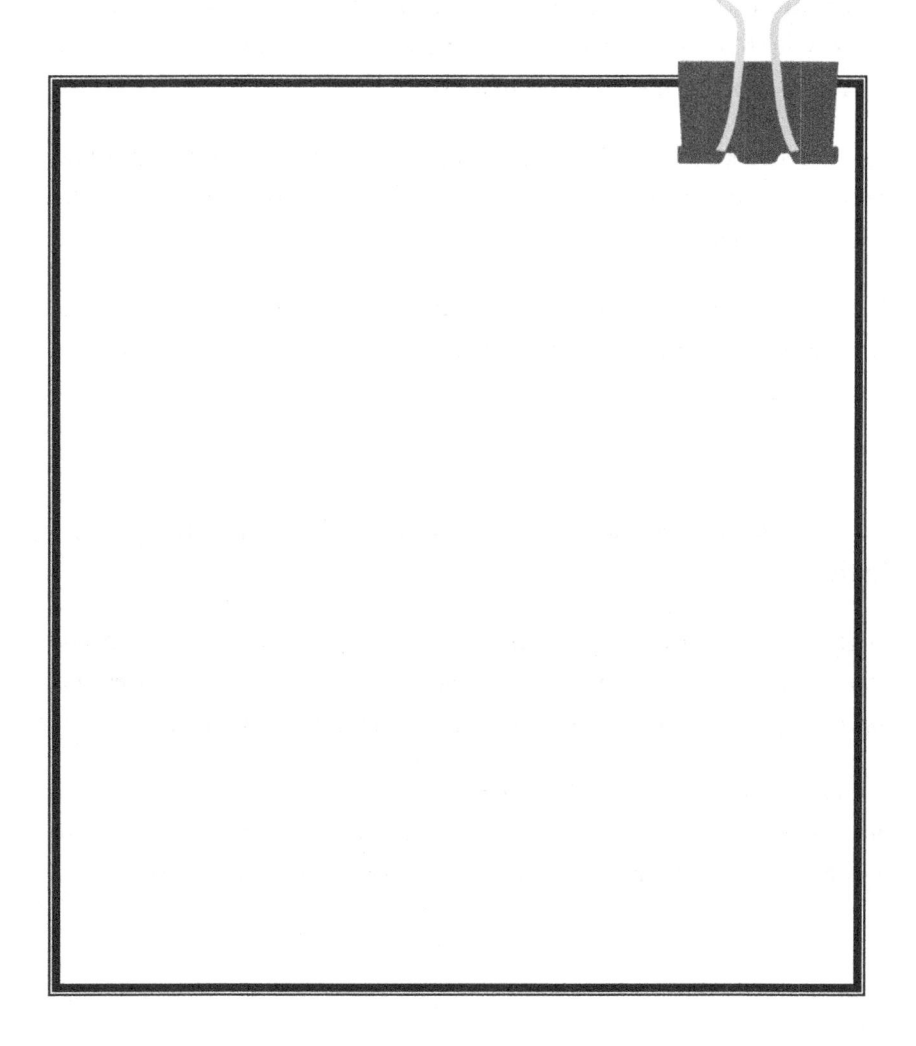

DAY 21 - Third reflection: What's taking up your time now?

Today you close the third week of the challenge. And it's time for you to ask yourself an essential question: What is now occupying the space that used to fill your cell phone?

During these days, you have learned to observe yourself, to reduce notifications, to turn off your cell phone at certain times... But this week you have done something even more important: you have started to replace one habit with another.

Because the key to any lasting change is not only in quitting a bad habit. It's in filling that void with something real, something valuable, something that makes you feel good.

Today it is time to stop and look at what has changed. What activities, emotions and relationships have reappeared when the screen stopped occupying everything.

🔖 Case study: Miguel, 45 years old - "I had time for myself again".

Miguel is an engineer, father of three children and a compulsive cell phone user. When he started this challenge, he told me that he had no time for anything, that he lived under stress, that he was always exhausted.

But in the third week, something changed. One day, in my office, he said to me: "I don't know what happened, but now I have time to read, to play with my children, to go for a run... And before I swore I didn't have time."

What had happened was both simple and profound: He had stopped giving away his time to his cell phone. And, in doing so, he had discovered that the day still had 24 hours, but now they belonged to him.

What has changed in your life?

You may have noticed things this week that you didn't see before:

- That you have more time than you thought.
- That your mind is clearer.
- That you have recovered activities that you had forgotten.
- That your relationships are more authentic when they are not filtered by a screen.

Today I invite you to observe these changes carefully. Because what you discover today will be the basis for consolidating the change in the last week.

🎯 Today's challenge

Today I want you to spend at least 20-30 minutes taking an honest stock of this week. You can write it down or simply reflect on these questions:

1. What new habits have you incorporated this week?
2. What activities have now taken up the time you used to spend on your cell phone?
3. What sensations have you experienced when you have recovered that time?
4. What relationship have you noticed between cell phone use and your emotional well-being?

5. What has been the most difficult for you this week and what has surprised you the most?

If you like, write down a small commitment for the week ahead: what real and meaningful activity do you want to continue to prioritize in your digital life?

Week 3 Summary: Replace the Habit

In this third week you have taken a decisive step in your digital detox. It was no longer just about turning off your cell phone. Now it was about filling the void that the screen had occupied for so long. **And you did it with courage.**

You have regained silence, movement, real conversations, contact with your body, your mindfulness...

And, most importantly, you've started to look inward. To hold your emotions without the need to escape to the screen.

This week has shown you that real life needs no filters, no notifications, no external validation. It just needs your presence.

What you have accomplished this week:

- You have learned to tolerate boredom without the need to cover it up with stimuli.
- You have stopped automatically reacting to every message or notification.
- You have reconnected with your body through conscious movement.
- You have regained mindfulness by walking, observing and being present.
- You've had real conversations, no cell phone involved.
- You've begun to identify what emotions you were trying to avoid with compulsive cell phone use... and you've begun to sustain them.

WEEK 4 - CONSOLIDATE THE CHANGE

Welcome to the last full week of this challenge.

You've traveled a path that, when you started, may have seemed impossible. Just a few weeks ago, you lived trapped in a loop of notifications, infinite scrolling and digital anxiety. Today, if you've made it this far, I'm sure you're no longer the same person.

But this is where the most important part begins.

It is not enough to be 30 days more conscious, more free, more in control of your time. Now it's time to make sure that this change is not temporary, but permanent.

Cell phone addiction does not disappear overnight. Like any habit, it can always come back, especially in times of stress, loneliness or boredom. That's why this week is designed to help you build the foundation for a healthy, balanced relationship with technology that will last beyond this challenge.

In these seven days you will:

- Learn to create lasting rules for yourself and your environment.

- Consolidate the new habits you have incorporated.

- Know how to manage the days when you relapse or lose focus.

- Recover essential spaces in your life: sleep, relationships, calm.

- Understand that this challenge was not a punishment, but a gift to yourself.

- Assume that the responsibility for maintaining this change is yours alone.

- Feeling proud of the road you have traveled and ready to move forward.

This week will not be a sprint. It will be the building of a firm foundation. Because there's no point in getting this far if you're back to square one in a few days. It's time to learn to live with technology differently. Not to give it up, but to make sure that it never again runs your life.

Now it's time to consolidate the change.

DAY 22 - Create your Digital Plan

Today we are going to build the bridge between what you have achieved and what you are going to maintain from now on

You've spent three weeks following a clear, guided path, with daily challenges. But life is not a 30-day challenge. Life goes on, with its rush, its problems, its temptations. And if you don't design a plan for after this book, if you don't decide how you want to relate to your cell phone, inertia will drag you back to the starting point.

That's why today we are going to create your **Personal Digital Plan**.

It will not be a set of rigid rules, nor a punishment. It will be an agreement with yourself, adapted to your life, to your priorities, to what you have learned. Because the difference between falling back or keeping the change is in having a plan.

What is a digital plan?

A digital plan is not a list of prohibitions. It is a set of conscious decisions about how you want technology to be present in your life.

It's up to you:

- Which applications are worth your attention and which are not.
- At what times of the day you want to be available and when you don't.
- Which spaces will be mobile-free.
- What habits you want to maintain in the long term.

🎯 **Real case: Patricia, 42 years old - "When I finished the challenge, everything came back".**

Patricia completed this same challenge a couple of years ago. She did it with discipline, with enthusiasm. She reached day 30 and was happy, convinced that she had overcome her addiction to her cell phone.

But she didn't make a plan for later. She didn't think about how to protect her time when he went back to work, when the vacations came, when life was full of unforeseen events again.

A few months later, she wrote to me, "I'm worse than before. The cell phone took up all my time again without me noticing."

We worked together again. This time, the first thing we did at the end of the challenge was to design her Personal Digital Plan. Today, two years later, she still maintains 80% of the changes she achieved then.

🎯 **Today's challenge**

Today I propose you to write your own Digital Plan. Spend at least 20 minutes to answer these questions and build your roadmap:

1. **At what times of the day do you want your cell phone not to be a part of your life?**
   (For example: upon awakening, during meals, before going to sleep).

2. **Which applications or social networks are you going to limit or eliminate permanently?**

(You can use control apps, set a specific time to consult them or, directly, delete them).

3. **What spaces in your home, work or social life do you declare a mobile-free zone?**
   (For example, the bedroom, the kitchen, the dining room, a restaurant...).

4. **What new habits do you want to keep from now on?**
   (Example: go for a walk without a cell phone, leave your cell phone in another room while you work, read every night, practice mindfulness...).

5. **How will you manage relapses?**
   (You can write down warning signs, actions to help you reconnect, or people to ask for help if you notice yourself slipping back into old habits).

Write it down clearly, briefly and visibly. This plan will be your anchor for when temptation returns, because it will return.

YOUR DIGITAL PLAN

93 - THE 30-DAY CHALLENGE

? **Question for reflection**

How do you think your life will change if you are faithful to this plan for the next six months?

DAY 23 - Turn off your cell phone for one hour a day.

Today we are going to take a decisive and symbolic step: turn off the cell phone consciously, by our own decision.

During these weeks, you have gradually regained control. You have reduced notifications, you have eliminated toxic apps, you have created mobile-free spaces. But surely, you still haven't allowed yourself to do something as simple and powerful as turning off your phone, even if only for a while.

Why? Because turning it off for real, even for an hour, confronts us with an uncomfortable feeling: that of being unavailable, of having no immediate refuge, of the world continuing to spin without us.

But that is precisely where true freedom begins.

When you are able to consciously turn off your cell phone, even if it is only for an hour a day, you are sending a clear message: "I am the one who decides".

📌 **Case in point: Sheryl Sandberg and conscious disconnection after pain.**

Sheryl Sandberg, known worldwide for being the COO of Facebook (Meta) for more than a decade and author of the bestseller Lean In, has been one of the most influential women in the tech world.

But she has also been one of the first figures in the digital world to publicly acknowledge the need to disconnect in order to reconnect with herself.

In 2015, Sheryl experienced a personal tragedy: the sudden death of her husband, Dave Goldberg. In the months that followed, she not only had to deal with the deepest grief, but also the emotional impact of being permanently exposed to a social network that, paradoxically, she had helped to build.

It was then that she made a drastic decision: to reduce her use of cell phones and networks to a minimum. Not just for pain. But for emotional survival.

In subsequent interviews, Sandberg has explained that during that process she learned something crucial:

"Social networks can give us company when we need it, but they can also prevent us from living the mourning, the silence, the reflection, the real connection. I had to learn to be with myself again, without hiding behind a screen."

She began to establish very concrete rules in his life:

- *Leave the cell phone out of the bedroom.*
- *Do not use during family meals.*
- *Mute notifications outside working hours.*
- *Set aside daily spaces without screens for reading, walking or just being with your children.*

In her second book, Option B, written with psychologist Adam Grant, Sheryl openly reflects on the importance of learning to sustain pain, discomfort, vulnerability... without fleeing to an immediate stimulus such as a cell phone.

Her story is a valuable lesson: Even someone who has been at the heart of the digital world has felt the need to disconnect in order to reconnect with her humanity.

🎯 Today's challenge

Today I'm going to ask you a challenge that I know is not easy. Choose a specific time of the day when you will turn off your cell phone completely.

During that hour:

- There will be no notifications, no calls, no networks, no distractions.

- You can dedicate yourself to whatever you want: reading, walking, playing sports, resting, being with someone.

- At the end of the hour, observe how you feel and whether something "urgent" has really happened.

❓ Question for reflection

What did you feel when you turned off your cell phone by choice? What changed in you during that hour? Did the world stop?

DAY 24 - Sleep without a cell phone

Today we are going to work on one of the most harmful -and most normalized- habits of the digital era: sleeping with your cell phone next to you.

You may not have thought about it, but the place where your cell phone sleeps says a lot about your relationship with it. If the first gesture you make when you open your eyes and the last one before going to sleep is to look at the screen, your rest and your mental health are paying a very high price.

Several studies have shown that having your cell phone on your bedside table negatively affects sleep quality, increases anxiety levels and fuels feelings of chronic fatigue. Notifications, blue light from the screen and the need to check "just in case" interrupt your rest and alter your natural rhythm. So-called circadian rhythms.

Today we are going to break that habit. Because the night is for resting, not for staying connected.

📌 Case in point: Arianna Huffington and her "cell phone box".

Arianna Huffington, founder of the Huffington Post and one of the most influential women in the media world, experienced firsthand the consequences of a hyper-connected life.

For years, she worked at a frenetic pace, getting little sleep, answering emails at all hours and convinced that productivity came before well-being.

Until, in 2007, she collapsed in his office. Literally. She collapsed from exhaustion and hit her head against his desk. That episode marked a before and after.

In her book "The Sleep Revolution," Huffington describes how that breakdown forced her to completely rethink her lifestyle, and particularly her relationship with her cell phone. She realized that lack of sleep - exacerbated by constant screen use - was not only undermining her health, but also her creativity, decision-making and happiness.

One of the habits she instituted was as symbolic as it was powerful: creating a "cell phone box" in her home, where every night she leaves his device before going to sleep.

She explains: "Not sleeping with my cell phone on my bedside table was one of the most liberating acts of my life. By leaving it out of the bedroom, I started to reclaim my nights... and also my mornings."

Huffington turned this gesture into a ritual:

- *Turn off the cell phone at least 30 minutes before going to bed.*
- *Place it in a specific box, outside the room.*
- *Replace the screen with a relaxing routine: a warm bath, light reading, mindful breathing or writing.*

For her, the quality of rest does not start when you close your eyes, but when you decide to turn off the digital world.

Today, in her talks and conferences, she continues to insist on a clear message: "Sleeping well is an investment. And keeping your cell phone away from your bed is the first smart decision you can make to get a better rest."

This simple gesture - putting your cell phone in a box every night - has become a symbol of digital self-care.

The quality of your rest is the quality of your life.

Your day doesn't start when the alarm goes off. Your day starts the night before, with the quality of your sleep. Sleeping without a cell phone will not only improve your rest. It will improve your mood, your concentration, your creativity and your ability to live the day from calm, not from urgency.

Today you are going to take a step that can change your life more than you can imagine.

🎯 Today's challenge

Tonight I want you to leave your cell phone out of the room. If you use it as an alarm clock, look for an analog clock. If you are afraid of something urgent happening, leave the volume on in another room, but away from you.

Tomorrow, observe how you slept and how you feel when you wake up.

❓ Question for reflection

How has your rest changed without your cell phone by your side? What did you notice in your mind and body when you woke up?

DAY 25 - An afternoon without a screen

Today we're going to really test ourselves. We're going to see how much control you've regained.

Throughout these weeks, we have been lowering the volume of your digital dependence: fewer notifications, fewer toxic apps, more moments without a cell phone, new activities that fill you up. But now it's time to try something that, when you started this challenge, would probably have seemed impossible: spending a whole afternoon without your cell phone.

Not to punish yourself. Not as an exercise of willpower. But for you to experience, in first person, what happens when you live several hours without interruptions, without distractions, without digital stimuli.

This afternoon will be a dress rehearsal of what your life can be like if you decide not to be a slave to the screen again.

📌 **Real case: Michael, 46 years old - "I discovered that I did not remember to live".**

Michael is a lawyer, father of two children and a compulsive cell phone user. He told me that he needed the phone all day long, that his work, his friends, his commitments demanded it.

When he reached this point in the challenge, I suggested that he spend an entire afternoon without his cell phone. He had a hard time accepting it. He postponed it several times. He would tell me, "I can't, I have things to attend to."

The day he finally did, he chose a Saturday. He turned his cell phone off at four o'clock in the afternoon and turned it on at eight o'clock. During those four hours, he went for a walk, had a black coffee, read for a while and played with his children in the park.

When we saw each other the following week, he told me, "I didn't know that in four hours I could fit so much life. I realized I had truly been present — really alive." From then on, Saturday afternoons without a cell phone became a sacred habit for him and his family.

What happens when you disconnect completely?

When you remove the option to consult your cell phone, something changes inside you:

- Your attention expands.
- Your mind calms down.
- Your relationships improve.
- Your thoughts are ordered.
- Time seems to stretch.

And you discover that real life was always there, waiting for you to look up.

🎯 Today's challenge

Choose an afternoon this week and spend at least 4 consecutive hours without a cell phone or screen.

Let them know if you need to (your family, someone who might need you). Use that time to do what you want to do: walk, read, cook, talk, be with yourself, be bored.

❓ Question for reflection

What has changed in you during these hours? What have you regained that you had lost long ago?

DAY 26 - Your first digital day off (if you choose to do so)

Today I pose one of the most powerful challenges of the whole process. A challenge that is not mandatory, but that can mark a before and after in your relationship with your cell phone: to live a whole day without a screen.

I know it may scare you. That, when you read this, your mind starts looking for excuses: *"I can't today. I have important things to attend to. It's impossible because of my work, my family, my commitments."*

I understand. But I want you to ask yourself an honest question: How indispensable are you really for a single day?

This challenge is not to see if you can live without a cell phone forever. It's for you to experience what a whole day feels like without relying on a device. For you to live a real day, like maybe you haven't lived for years.

And if you decide not to do it today, that's okay. But I want you to try it at least once in the next few weeks. Because the experience is worth it.

📌 **Case history: Martha, 29 years old - "The best Sunday in years".**

Martha is a graphic designer who had fallen into a familiar pattern: every Sunday morning she told herself she was going to unplug, but by the afternoon, she would find herself glued to her phone—scrolling endlessly, with that sinking feeling that the weekend had slipped away.

When she reached this point in the challenge, she told me that it was impossible for her to go a whole day without looking at her cell phone. I suggested that she try it on a Sunday, letting her family and friends know beforehand that she would be "unplugged".

She did. The next day she wrote to me: "It had been years since I had such a long day, so peaceful and so much my own. I was with my parents, I cooked, I went for a walk, I finished a book. When I turned my cell phone back on, the world was still there. But I had found myself again."

From then on, Martha established a free digital Sunday every month.

What happens when the screen disappears?

Things happen during a free digital day that you may have forgotten about:

- Time dilates.
- Your mind calms down.
- Your attention returns to the present moment.
- Conversations are deeper.
- You realize how much noise you had normalized.
- You don't need to go to the countryside or do anything extraordinary. You just need to turn off the screen and live the day as you did before.

🎯 Today's challenge

If you feel ready, choose a day (today or during this week) to make your first digital day free: Turn off your cell phone from the moment you wake up until you go to bed. Let whoever you feel necessary know in advance.

❓ Question for reflection

What did it feel like to live a whole day without a cell phone? What did you recover that you had lost? How do you want to use this discovery moving forward?

DAY 27 - Learn to manage relapses

Today we are going to talk about something unavoidable: stumbles.

Because, even if you reach day 30, even if you finish this challenge successfully, there will be days when you will fall again. Days in which, without realizing it, you will compulsively unlock the screen again. And that doesn't mean you've failed. It means you are human.

The important thing is not to avoid relapses at all costs. The important thing is to know what to do when they happen. Because the real change is not in never falling, but in learning to get up every time you stumble.

Today I want to teach you how to manage those moments so that they don't erase everything you have achieved.

📌 **Case in point: Demi Lovato. Falling down, coming to terms with it and getting back up again**

Demi Lovato is an internationally recognized artist: singer, actress and activist. But beyond her public career, she has also been one of the most open and courageous figures to talk about her mental health issues, addictions and relapses.

From a very young age, Demi lived with eating disorders, depression, anxiety and substance abuse. She entered rehab for the first time when she was only 18 years old. And for a while, she managed to stay sober, strong, and committed to her process.

But in 2018, after six years of sobriety, she relapsed and began using again. Not long after, she suffered an overdose that nearly took her life.

What he did next is what makes her story a powerful example: she didn't hide the relapse. She didn't sink into guilt. She decided to tell it. With honesty. With rawness. And with courage that few dare to show.

In the documentary "Dancing with the Devil", Demi tells her story in first person. She does not seek to give lessons. She seeks to show what almost nobody tells:

"Relapsing made me feel like I had failed. That everything I had accomplished was for nothing. But I learned that a relapse doesn't erase your path. It just reminds you that you need to keep taking care of yourself."

Since then, she has continued to work on her recovery process, adapting her life, her environment, her habits. She recognizes that she is still struggling. That she doesn't have all the answers. But she also leaves a clear message:

"I am not weak for having relapsed. I am strong for getting back on my feet."

What to do when you relapse?

These are the keys I want you to integrate today:

- Detect the warning signs. Start observing what situations, emotions or routines lead you to compulsively look at your cell phone again. Stress, tiredness, boredom, loneliness... These are moments of risk.

- Don't beat yourself up. A relapse is not a failure. It is an opportunity to learn what you need to reinforce.

- Go back to your Digital Plan. Reread it, review your rules, remember why you started this challenge.

- Activate an "emergency plan". Have a list of actions ready for those difficult days: go for a walk, call a friend, turn off your cell phone for an hour, practice mindfulness, exercise.

- Ask for help if you need it. Share your experience with someone you trust. Talking about it always helps to put it into perspective.

🎯 Today's challenge

Today, design your own Anti-Relapse Plan.

Write down the answers to these questions:

- What are the signs that you are falling back into excessive cell phone use?

- What emotions or situations tend to trigger these relapses?

- What will you do when you detect that you have relapsed (concrete actions)?

- Who could you turn to for support?

This plan is not a punishment. It is a tool to take care of you.

111 - THE 30-DAY CHALLENGE

? Question for reflection

What have you learned from your previous relapses in life? What have they taught you about your ability to get back on your feet?

DAY 28 - Fourth reflection: This is not about cell phones, it's about you.

You've reached the end of week four. And if anything has become clear over the past few days, it's that this challenge was never just about screens.

It was about you.

About how you treat yourself. About how you take care of your time, your mind, your relationships, your body. About how you have learned not to run away, not to react, not to depend.

This week has been different from the previous ones. More silent, more intimate. It has been the stage where you have stopped fighting with your cell phone... and you have started to live with a different consciousness.

You've slept better. You've dedicated real time to you, without filters. You've turned off the screen to turn on what matters. And you've felt what it means to be present.

Today there is no new technique and no new challenge. I just want you to look back and observe all that you have accomplished. Not in an idealized way. Not as something perfect. But as the courageous and human process that it has been.

🌶 Real case: Peter, 50 years old - "I thought this was for young people... until I saw myself reflected".

When Peter came to the office and I proposed the 30-day digital detox challenge, he looked at me as if I were an alien.

At first he saw it as something "juvenile, modern". However, in the third week, he realized something that changed his outlook: "I had also been running away from myself for years with my cell phone. I didn't realize it until I saw myself having dinner alone, in front of a screen, ignoring the person sitting right across from me."

Today, Peter no longer sleeps with his cell phone next to him. He walks alone, without headphones. And he has gotten back into the habit of calling his friends to talk, instead of just sending memes.

"This has not been a digital challenge. It's been a reconciliation with me."

What have you really learned?

Today I want to leave you with some questions to close this week with a broader view:

- What have you discovered about yourself during this month?
- What emotions have you learned to hold without the need for a screen?
- What spaces, habits or relationships have you recovered?
- What have you gained by living with fewer distractions?
- What part of you has awakened since the cell phone stopped taking up everything?

🎯 Today's challenge

Take at least 20 minutes today to write (or calmly think about) a letter addressed to the person you were before you started this challenge.

It doesn't matter if the letter is short or long. The important thing is that you recognize your process. That you validate your effort and that you leave proof that something has changed.

❓ Question for reflection

Who are you now that you no longer need to look at the screen every moment?

Which version of you do you want to continue to nurture from today?

Week 4 Summary - Consolidate the change

You reached the fourth week of the challenge. And it wasn't just another week: it was the decisive step to transform what you have learned into a lifestyle.

During these days you have not made big, radical changes. You have done something more difficult, more courageous and more profound: sustaining change. You've stabilized what you had already started to build. Turn a 30-day experiment into a real commitment to you.

Because anyone can disconnect from their cell phone for a while. But transforming your way of living, of sleeping, of looking, of being... Only those who dare to look inward can do it.

What you have accomplished this week:

- You have designed your own Personal Digital Plan, adapted to your real life.

- You have practiced voluntary disconnection for an hour, an afternoon or even a whole day.

- You have regained a real rest, without a screen before going to sleep.

- You have learned that relapses are not the end, but a natural part of the journey, and you have prepared your Emergency Plan for when they come.

- You have become aware of the impact your example can have on others.

- You closed the week with a deep reflection on who you are now and what you have gained by living with fewer distractions.

🎯 What you should take away from this week:

This week has taught you that you don't need to check your cell phone every minute to live freely. What you need is to be clear about your internal compass. Remember why you started. And know that you have a choice.

You have learned to respect your limits, to say "this far", to prioritize your attention. You've realized that the world doesn't fall apart if you turn off your cell phone. And that life - the real life - becomes sharper, kinder, deeper when you look up.

What's next?

Now the last stretch remains.

The 29th will be your commitment to the future.

On the 30th, your celebration and your look forward to what is to come.

DAY 29 - The Power to Inspire Others

You've reached day 29. And today we're not just going to talk about you.
Today we're going to talk about the impact your change can have on the world around you.

Maybe you started this challenge thinking it was something personal. That you were doing it for you, for your mental health, to get your time back. And it is true, you have done it for you. But what you probably had not imagined is that this process you are living has a contagious effect.

When someone close to you - your partner, your child, your friend, your co-worker - sees that something has changed in you, they can't help but wonder, "How did he do it?" "Could I do it too?"

That is the true power of change: when it transforms your life, it begins to transform the lives of others as well.

🌸 Known case: Emma Watson and the mirror effect

Emma Watson, British actress, women's rights activist and UN ambassador, has been a public figure in the media for years.

But unlike many celebrities of her generation, she has also been one of the first to publicly question the constant exposure, digital noise and pressure to always be connected.

In various interviews, Emma has told how, despite working in an industry obsessed with image and visibility, she has made a conscious decision to protect her time, attention and mental health.

"I have learned to value silence, moments without stimuli, evenings without notifications. Disconnection is not a luxury, it's a necessity."

Instead of sharing every moment of her life in networks, Emma cultivates habits that often go unnoticed... but that transform inside:

- *Turn off the cell phone for several hours a day.*
- *Spend time reading paper books.*
- *She writes by hand as a form of introspection.*
- *She goes for a walk without headphones, alone with her thoughts.*
- *Choose not to expose yourself to digital overstimulation, even if it means "missing out."*

In a recent speech, she reflected on his decision to lead a "quieter" life, away from the constant bombardment of the networks:

"We've been taught that to be disconnected is to lose relevance. But I believe that to be too connected is to lose depth."

Her example, although silent, is profoundly powerful. Because it shows that there is no need to preach, no need to convince, no need to give lessons. It is enough to live differently. And when you do, others notice.

Change does not end with you

I want you to understand something important: Your transformation is not an individual matter. We are trapped in a world that normalizes hyperconnectedness, digital anxiety, technological dependence. Every person who breaks that chain is opening a crack in that system.

When you regain control, you are showing others that they can do it too.

Maybe your kids start to question their habits. Maybe your partner is encouraged to try an evening without a cell phone. Maybe a friend asks you how you did it.

And there begins a new cycle of change.

You are already the proof that it can be done. Now you can be the inspiration.

🎯 Today's challenge

Today, I want you to go one step further:

- Think of someone close to you who you think could benefit from this challenge.

- Write them a sincere message, tell them about your experience, share what you have learned, invite them to read this book or start their own process.

- Don't try to convince. Just share your story, your path, what you have discovered.

Also, answer these questions in writing or mentally:

Who in your environment could initiate this change thanks to you?

What impact would it have on your life and your relationship?

What have you learned in these weeks that you would like to pass on to that person?

? Question for reflection

What seed can you plant in the world today from your own transformation?

DAY 30 - Choose your new life, every day

You made it.

You have reached the end of the challenge. But this is not the end of anything. It is the beginning of a new way of living.

Today you don't need a challenge. Today you need a decision. The decision not to turn back. The decision to take care of your time, your attention, your rest, your presence. To remember that your life is worth more than any notification.

During these 30 days you have done something very difficult in this digital age: you have left the autopilot. You have learned to look inward. You have discovered that you can live without depending on a screen. And that is an act of freedom.

◆ Case in point: Rafa Nadal and the power of silent repetition.

Rafa Nadal, one of the most admired athletes of all time, is not the fastest, nor the most technical, nor the most mediatic. But there is one thing that defines him above all else: his consistency.

During an interview, someone asked him how he maintained discipline every day, even when there was no audience, no cameras, no major tournaments. And his answer was simple and powerful:

"I train the same way on a Monday morning with no one watching me as I do on center court at Roland Garros. Because commitment is not shown when everything goes well. It shows when no one is watching you.

That is exactly what you have done in these 30 days.

- You chose to turn off your cell phone when no one was forcing you to.
- You have learned to hold uncomfortable emotions without running away.
- You have said "no" to distractions to say "yes" to you.

And that, even if no one sees it, even if you don't share it on networks, is a giant victory.

Don't expect to be perfect. Expect to be conscious.

As of tomorrow, there will be no instructions. There will be no "31st day". There will be good days and difficult days. There will be moments of relapse, of automatism, of temptation. And there will also be moments of clarity, of calm, of real connection. The key is not not to fail.

The key is to remember:

- Remember that you have a choice.
- Remember that your attention is valuable.
- Remember that you set the pace of your life, not the screen.

🎯 Today's challenge

Today, do nothing.

Just sit with yourself, without your phone, for 10 minutes.

Think about everything you've done this month. All that you have felt, let go of, and recovered. And when you're done, say out loud, even in a whisper: "I decide. I choose. And today I choose to live present."

Final thought: Life begins when you turn off the screen.

Maybe right now you're not fully aware of all that you've accomplished. But let me remind you: A month ago, you were stuck in a routine you didn't choose. You lived pending notifications, the approval of others, constant stimuli that stole your attention and your energy. You had become accustomed to living with your head bent toward a screen, believing that there was no other way to live.

But you decided there was. You decided to start this challenge. And for 30 days, step by step, you have learned to recover something you had lost: **Your time. Your attention. Your life.**

This is not the end. It is the beginning. Nothing ends today. Today is the beginning of everything. This challenge was not a 30-day challenge. It was a training for life. From now on, you decide how you use your time. You decide when to turn on and when to turn off the screen.
You decide how you want to live.

And most importantly: now you know you can.

A final thought

You haven't unhooked from your phone — you've reconnected with yourself.

And that doesn't last 30 days. It lasts a lifetime.

Thank you for daring.

Thank you for supporting us.

Thank you for being here, really.

See you in the real world.

PART THREE – RESOURCES TO HELP YOU MOVE FORWARD

THE CHALLENGE IS OVER... BUT THE ROAD CONTINUES.

If you're reading this, you've reached the end of the challenge. And I want you to stop for a second to celebrate. Because what you've done is not easy.

You have been brave. You have looked a socially accepted addiction in the face, you have changed habits that you had been carrying around for years and you have regained control over something that was stealing your life.

But now the most important part begins: maintaining that change.

Because digital addiction doesn't go away. The temptation will always be there, in your pocket, on your desk, on your bedside table. And if you are not attentive, if you do not take care of what you have achieved, little by little, without you realizing it, the cell phone will return to occupy the center of your life.

That's why I wanted to include this third part. Here you won't find any more challenges. What you will find are tools, resources, reminders and strategies to make this change lasting.

You've completed your training. Now the real game begins. And I want you to have everything you need to win.

YOUR MAINTENANCE PLAN

What is a maintenance plan?

Over the past few weeks, you have made a conscious effort to change. You've followed guidelines, you've completed challenges, you've reflected on yourself. But real life is chaotic, unpredictable, full of excuses and temptations.

A maintenance plan is not a set of rigid rules. It is an agreement with yourself, a compass for when you lose your way, a lifeline for when things get out of control.

Here I propose a basic plan. You can adapt it to your life, add or remove what you need. The important thing is not to forget that the control is in your hands.

Essential rules for your digital life

- **Don't start the day with your cell phone.**

    The first hour of the day is for you, not for notifications. Don't check social media, email or messages until after you've had breakfast, showered, and started your actual day.

- **Do not use your cell phone before going to sleep.**

    The last hour of the day is for rest. Read, talk, write, breathe... but don't let the last image you see be a screen.

- **Establish mobile-free zones.**

    The dining room, the bedroom, family gatherings... let there be spaces where the cell phone does not enter.

- **Disable unnecessary notifications.**

   Only important calls and messages. Everything else can wait.

- **Check your usage time every month.**

   Spend five minutes, once a month, looking at how much time you have spent in front of the screen and on which apps. Be honest with yourself.

- **Keep making digital days or afternoons free.**

   Even if you have already completed the challenge, continue to set aside time to completely disconnect.

- **Keep cultivating your new habits.**

   The activities you discovered during the challenge (reading, walking, sports, mindfulness...) should continue to take priority over your cell phone.

The digital traffic light: detecting your warning signs

To help you detect when you are starting to regress, I suggest you use this traffic light system:

GREEN HABITS (the ones you want to keep):

- Turn off the cell phone during meals.
- Do not use the cell phone when waking up or before going to sleep.
- Check notifications only at specific times.
- Practice screen-free activities every day.

YELLOW HABITS (risky, require attention):

- Going back to looking at your cell phone when you go to bed.
- Consult social networks more than 30 minutes a day.
- Feeling anxious when you do not have your cell phone nearby.
- Use the cell phone as a refuge to avoid uncomfortable emotions.

RED HABITS (alert, you're going backwards):

- Spending more than 3 hours a day on social networks.
- Using the cell phone at the table, in bed or in meetings.
- Feeling that you can't be alone without your cell phone.
- Stop practicing the newly acquired habits.

If you detect that you have returned to yellow or red habits, go back through this book. Go back to your plan. Remind yourself of your reasons — and take action.

USEFUL RESOURCES

You've already done a great job during these 30 days. But I know that daily life is demanding, that digital temptation is always there, and that sometimes you need extra support.

Therefore, in this chapter you will find a selection of resources to help you stay on track when you feel you may lose control again.

These are tools you can use as a complement to everything you've learned. They're not a magic solution—because the key will always be within you—but they can be great allies in your day-to-day life.

▦ Apps to control the use of cell phones

If you want to keep an eye on your screen time, these apps may be useful:

Digital Wellbeing (Android) / Screen Time (iOS):

Integrated into your operating system. They show you how many hours you use your phone, which apps you consume the most, and allow you to set time limits.

Forest:

As long as you don't use your phone, a virtual tree grows. If you unlock it too soon, the tree dies. A fun and visual way to motivate yourself to disconnect.

Freedom:

Allows you to block distractions on your cell phone and computer during the hours you choose.

Offtime:

Create profiles (work, family, leisure) and limit access to certain apps and notifications according to the time of day.

Quality Time:

It gives you detailed reports on how much time you spend on your mobile and alerts you when you exceed your own limits.

📚 Recommended books

If you want to continue learning and going deeper about digital addiction, time management and habits, these books can help you:

📖 **Atomic Habits - James Clear**: a clear and practical book on how habits work and how to change them.

📖 **Ten Arguments for Deleting Your Social Media Accounts Right Now - Jaron Lanier**: an in-depth analysis of how social networks affect our mental health.

📖 **The Happiness Trap - Russ Harris**: doesn't talk directly about digital addiction, but it will help you understand how the constant search for stimuli takes us away from real life.

🎥 Recommended documentaries

If you prefer to watch rather than read, these documentaries will open your eyes to the digital industry and its mechanisms:

🎬 **"The Social Dilemma" (Netflix):** an X-ray of how social networks are designed to capture our attention and manipulate our behavior.

🎬 **"The Great Hack" (Netflix):** an analysis on data manipulation and how social networks affect our decisions without us knowing it.

🧘 Complementary techniques

During the challenge, we have worked a lot on reflection and observation, but here are some other practices that can help you keep your balance:

- **Mindfulness:**

  Spend 5-10 minutes a day breathing, observing your thoughts and connecting with yourself without distractions.

- **Journaling (conscious writing):**

  Write down every day how you feel, what you have done, what you want to improve. Writing it down will help you stay focused.

- **Daily physical activity:**

  Sport and movement are great allies to reduce anxiety and the desire to seek digital stimuli.

- **Programmed digital disconnection:**

    Set aside fixed times during the week to turn off your cell phone (afternoons, Sundays, evenings...) and stick to them as if it were an unavoidable appointment.

Remember: these tools are not an end in themselves. They are just that: tools. The real transformation has been initiated by you during these 30 days. But now you have the resources to keep that change growing.

QUICK GUIDE FOR PARENTS: HOW TO HELP YOUR CHILDREN UNWIND

If you are reading this chapter, you probably didn't do this challenge just for yourself. Maybe you also started thinking about your children, worried about seeing them always with their heads tilted towards the screen, isolated, distracted, hooked.

And let me tell you something important: your concern is legitimate. Because this addiction does not only affect adults. Teenagers and children are, in many cases, the main victims of the digital age.

Their brains are still developing, and constant exposure to the cell phone affects their attention, self-esteem, relationships and emotional well-being.

But the good news is that you can be part of the change. Not with lectures. Not with punishments. But with example, guidance, and clear rules.

What you should know before you start

Your son or daughter was born into a hyperconnected world. For them, the cell phone is not a tool: it is part of their identity, their relationships, their way of communicating.

That means:

- It does no good to demonize technology.
- Prohibiting does not work. It generates rebellion and distance.
- What makes the difference is conscious accompaniment and real example.

If you can't put your cell phone down on the table, don't expect them to do it. If you can't do without a screen before bedtime, don't expect them to give it up.

So, before you talk to them, start with you. When they see you change, it will be much easier for them to want to follow you.

---

5 essential rules you can establish at home

Here are some simple but effective guidelines to make your children's digital lives healthier:

1. **Mobile-free zones:**
   Declare the dining table, bedroom and study time as screen-free spaces for all members of the household.

2. **Conscious digital timetable:**
   Establish time slots when the cell phone is not allowed (e.g., during meals, before bedtime, in the morning when waking up).

3. **Agreed time of use:**
   Negotiate with your children a daily time limit for the use of social networks, games or videos. Don't impose, agree. And stick to it yourself.

4. **Activities without screens:**
   Encourage alternative activities: sports, reading, games, walks, conversation, hobbies. The best way to reduce digital time is to fill real life with content.

5. **Open and sincere conversation:**
   Don't talk to them out of prohibition, but out of concern. Explain the risks, share your experience with this challenge and explain why you have also decided to change.

How to talk to your children without attacking them

Many parents make the mistake of approaching this issue with anger or censure. But the key is empathy and honesty.

You can start the conversation like this:

"I know that nowadays we are all hooked on the cell phone. I've been hooked too and have decided to change. I'd like us to talk about how we can live better, all together, without the screen taking up so much of our time and energy."

Involve them. Ask them how they feel, if they also notice that they are wasting time, if they would like to do something different.

And, above all, lead by example. There is nothing more powerful than seeing a parent turn off their cell phone to be present.

👪 Family activities to reinforce change

Here are some simple activities to reconnect with your children away from screens:

- One afternoon a week without cell phones for everyone.
- Board games.
- A walk, a hike, a board game or a special dinner without technology.
- A monthly "digital challenge" afternoon: see who can go the longest without touching their cell phone.
- Read this book together and propose that they also do the challenge adapted to their age.

Remember, your children don't need you to take away their cell phones. They need you to teach them how to live without depending on it. And that starts with your own example.

If you can change, so can they.

WHAT YOU SHOULD NEVER FORGET

This is the end of the book. But it is not the end of the road.

You have gone through a difficult, uncomfortable, sometimes even painful process.
You've looked your mobile addiction in the face, you've made changes, you've stepped out of your comfort zone.

And if there's one thing I want you to take away from this whole journey, it's this: The real goal of this challenge was never for you to put down your cell phone. The goal was to get you back to owning your time, your attention, your life.

Therefore, I want you to end this book with a series of essential reminders.

Short, clear sentences that you can reread every time you feel you are going backwards.

Phrases that will bring you back to the present and remind you why you started this journey.

What you should never forget

- The cell phone is a tool, not a refuge. It is not meant to calm your fears, your boredom or your loneliness. Use your cell phone. Don't let the cell phone use you.

- You are not indispensable 24 hours a day. The world doesn't end when you turn off the screen. Real life happens when you look up.

- Every minute you spend looking at a screen, you take away from something or someone. From your family, from your friends, from your dreams, from yourself.

- Digital addiction doesn't go away, it will always be lurking, but now you have the tools to avoid falling back into it.

- Disconnection is an act of self-love. Not to isolate yourself, but to reconnect with yourself and those around you.

- Freedom is not doing what you want when you want. Freedom is being able to decide. And now you can decide.

- You have not done this challenge just for you. You have done it for the people who love you, for those who look up to you and follow your example, for those who don't yet know they can be free.

- Life begins when you turn off the screen. Don't forget that.

THIS IS AS FAR AS WE HAVE COME

If you are reading these lines, it means that you have walked a brave path. You have gone through easy days and uncomfortable days. You have questioned habits that you have been carrying for years.

You have stopped. You have felt. You have chosen.

And that deserves all my respect.

When I started writing this book, I did it thinking of all the people who, like me, have ever felt trapped by a screen. I did it thinking about my children, my mother, my patients, and also you.

I didn't intend to give you a magic solution. I just wanted to offer you a map, a guide, a voice to accompany you as you rediscovered yourself.

And now, as I close this book, I want to tell you something important:

You can go on. You know how. You are capable.

This is not the end. It is an open door. A freer life, more connected to the real, more conscious... is waiting for you.

I wish you quality time. True moments. Silences filled with peace. Relationships that look each other in the eye. Days that are not counted in notifications, but in memories.

And if you ever get lost, you know the way back: start by turning off the screen, and coming back to you.

After so many days together, I dare to ask you a small favor. I want you to help me help more people who, like you and me, need to improve their relationship with their cell phone. To do so, I ask you for an honest review on Amazon, that way we will reach more people who need it. As we did on the 29th, we will inspire many more people.

Thank you for allowing us to walk with you over these 30 days. It has been an honor to be with you.

Turn off the cell phone.

Go out into the street.

Look at the sky, the people, the real world.

And remember that you already know how to live without relying on a screen.

The rest is up to you.

Violeta.

NOTES AND REFLECTIONS

Made in the USA
Monee, IL
10 July 2025